FUN WITH SCIENCE
46 Entertaining Demonstrations

George Barr

Illustrated by
Mildred Waltrip

DOVER PUBLICATIONS, INC.
New York

To Mom,
always
my best audience

The illusion on page 86 is adapted from an article by A. Ames, Jr., in *Psychological Monographs*, Volume 65, Number 324, "Visual Perception and the Rotating Trapezoidal Window."

Copyright

Published in Canada by General Publishing Company, Ltd., 30 Lesmill Road, Don Mills, Toronto, Ontario.
Published in the United Kingdom by Constable and Company, Ltd., 3 The Lanchesters, 162–164 Fulham Palace Road, London W6 9ER.

Bibliographical Note

This Dover edition, first published in 1994, is an unaltered and unabridged republication of the work first published in 1965 by McGraw-Hill Book Company, New York, under the title *Show Time for Young Scientists: Entertaining with Science.*

Library of Congress Cataloging-in-Publication Data

Barr, George, 1907–
    [Show time for young scientists]
    Fun with science : 46 entertaining demonstrations / George Barr ; illustrated by Mildred Waltrip.
        p.   cm.
    Originally published: Show time for young scientists. New York : McGraw-Hill, 1965.
    Includes index.
    ISBN 0-486-28000-4 (pbk.)
    1. Science—Experiments—Juvenile literature. 2. Scientific recreations—Juvenile literature. [1. Scientific recreations.] I. Waltrip, Mildred, ill. II. Title.
Q164.B34   1993
793.8—dc20   93–45547
                                                                        CIP
                                                                         AC

Manufactured in the United States of America
Dover Publications, Inc., 31 East 2nd Street, Mineola, N.Y. 11501

Introduction

As a young scientist you often perform certain demonstrations that amaze and entertain you. There is a tingle of excitement as you show them to the first person you see. At the beginning, you explain the "miracles" to your delighted family. Then you let some of your friends watch and marvel.

In time your groups become larger and larger. Before you know it, you may find yourself working before a big audience. Now you have become a popular entertainer, self-confident and capable of fascinating people with extraordinary scientific mysteries.

This book provides many ideas for spectacular presentations in science. It tells how to do these in a dramatic, enjoyable manner to arouse everybody's interest.

There is a technique for entertaining with science. The following chapters will give tips on professional-style showmanship. This will help you command maximum attention and afford great pleasure for your spectators. You will learn how to spice your acts with humor, if you are so inclined.

Special attention is devoted to the improvement of visibility. That is why everything is made large. Complete instructions are given for building the demonstration materials. These devices are kept simple. Only safe, easily available, or inexpensive articles are needed.

Many different scientific themes are covered, so that you can put together a well-balanced assembly show. There are also included scientific stunts and practical jokes for showing to individuals or small groups, such as clubs and parties. You may even use some ideas for science fairs or for further experimental research. The last chapter will tell you how to put on many different kinds of science shows.

Here are just a few unusual presentations you will learn to execute:

Bring a toy dog automatically out of a doghouse when you blow a horn!

Create an unbelievable illusion of a window flapping back and forth, when all the time you are turning it in one direction!

Mysteriously balance on the point of a stick the tips of giant paper butterflies and birds!

Do fascinating experiments with sound for a large audience while using a microphone as a big ear!

Turn over a glass of milk, while the fluid defies gravity and stays in the glass!

Stop the pulse in your wrist, at will!

And now—on with the show!

Contents

OPTICAL ILLUSIONS

SOUND

GRAVITY

ENTERTAINING SMALL GROUPS

PRACTICAL JOKES

OTHER TYPES OF SCIENCE SHOWS

Let's talk about showmanship

Have you ever gone to an enjoyable show where you sat spellbound on the edge of your seat, while you followed the words and movements of an excellent performer? During these keenly pleasurable moments you seemed to forget about the outside world. You were forced to give all your attention to what was happening on the stage. The performer was using a skill called showmanship. This is the ability to present something so that it makes a dramatic impact on the audience.

Good presentation is an important part of each science show. The finest demonstration can be ruined by poor technique. On the other hand, a very simple exhibition can be turned into something so exciting that your audience will be awaiting your next move eagerly and reacting to your remarks.

In this book you will discover that there are certain common-sense pointers used by successful demonstrators. Follow these suggestions as often as you can, and you too will be on the road toward becoming an exciting and welcome science showman.

Difference between a magic and a science show

A magician aims to mystify the audience. Accordingly, he uses all kinds of tricks to fool people. We forgive him even though we know that he may be using secret pockets to hide things. We only half-believe most of his remarks, because we feel that they are said to mislead us. We suspect that things on the stage are seldom what they seem. But we enjoy matching our wits against his —even though we are almost always the losers!

However, the purpose of your science show is not to fool people. By means of your interesting demonstration you are going to clarify some scientific principle in a dramatic and humorous manner. So you select unusual, and often startling, things to show. Then when you have everybody's attention, you can explain the scientific facts involved.

It is a wonderful way to teach the fascinating story of science. But you must be sure that your explanations are accurate, attention-holding, *and above all entertaining*.

The audience must be made to understand that an effect which seems like magic really has a very logical explanation. Sensible people know that everything happens for a reason. A scientist would say that every effect has a cause. Sometimes the cause is not very obvious.

For entertainment value you may play with the audience, and keep them waiting for the answer for a little while. You may even encourage them to think a bit and make a few guesses. But, even though the temptation is there, *never keep the secret from the audience.*

Remember, a science show need never be dull. For many people the true explanation may often sound like a miracle of magic. And indeed, it often does!

VISIBILITY—CAN EVERYBODY SEE?

It is obvious that if you want your audience to give you all its attention, then you must always be certain that *everybody* can see what is happening up front. If heads are in the way, and if the lights are dim, or the apparatus is too small, you will not be getting the most from your presentation.

Whenever possible, stand on an elevated platform or stage. If this setup is not available, you may have to look around for some way of raising the demonstration table. In an ordinary room the table can be raised by placing equal piles of books under each leg. Or you can keep your equipment on a board, or stiff material which is laid over some books or boxes on the table. Frequently an overturned empty carton, set on a table, provides a high working area.

To avoid having rows of people sitting behind other people, you can sometimes rearrange the chairs. If possible make a large three-quarter or semicircle, so everybody is facing you. If more rows are needed, place the next row of chairs so that people can see through the spaces left by the chairs in front.

Sometimes if the room is crowded, some people may not be able to see the table. In such a case you should hold the objects up high whenever possible. Remember too that the viewing angle makes a difference. So if you are showing something, turn from one side to the other so that everybody gets a full view.

Do this *slowly*, calling attention to what you wish the audience to observe carefully. A good performer is aware that some people are slower than others and that time must be allowed for things to "sink in."

The kind of background also makes a difference in how well things can be seen. If you hold a white object up against a white wall, then the visibility is decreased because there is no contrast. You should also not hold a black object against a black or dimly lighted background. It is easier to see white against a black background or vice versa.

Lighting is another very important condition to consider for visibility. There is nothing more dismal than a dimly illuminated demonstration table. Psychologists have performed interesting experiments to show that the spirits of an audience are immediately raised as the performing area becomes bathed with more light. Professionals are well aware of this, and that is why theaters have very bright spotlights. For greater contrast audiences also usually sit in the dark.

In the daytime you can throw more light on a table in a room simply by pulling up all the shades. Sunlight is a very powerful source of illumination—much more than electric lights.

At other times, whenever more light is needed, arrange to have spotlights shine on the table. Most homes and schools have clamp-on reflectors. Some living-room lamps can also be used to light up your demonstrations. You may even try the beam of a slide projector. This serves as a splendid spotlight.

Another practical way to increase visibility, if it is not possible to get your audience closer, is to use larger materials. If you hold up a sign to be read, then make sure that it can be read from the last seat. For a small group, it may be sufficient to use small apparatus. But for a larger audience, you can usually find larger sizes of the same items.

For example, instead of a handball, you can often use a basketball. A large glass or quart jar is more visible than a juice glass. For big audiences, avoid using small equipment, such as match sticks, pennies, or marbles.

Many demonstrators have learned how to enlarge certain small items and movements by producing shadows. A strong light in a reflector or a table lamp, will cast an enlarged shadow of an object on a screen, bed sheet, or wall.

The beam from a projector makes excellent shadows. Find the best place to hold your demonstration material to make the sharpest shadows of the desired size. If you use suitable material you may even have an entire show of "shadow science." Learn to make some interesting shadowgraphs with your fingers or cardboard cutouts. In this way you can introduce an element of humor in your shows.

PRACTICE—PRACTICE—PRACTICE

PRACTICE BEFORE A MIRROR

KEEP A NOTEBOOK

Even with the simplest demonstration it is always best to go through the routine several times without an audience. Things seldom work well the first time, for all kinds of reasons which you cannot anticipate.

Often the effect of a demonstration may not be good enough to suit you, even though it seemed so spectacular when you first thought of it. Then again, you may luckily discover that the dry cells are too weak, or that there are bad connections in your wiring, or that the electric bell is temperamental. You may find out just in time

16

that the balloon leaks, or that a piece of apparatus keeps falling over because it needs a broader base.

During practice you must do everything *exactly* as you will be doing it while performing. (Beware of unrehearsed, sudden changes when you are before a group.) Go through each motion, and consider visibility, where you will stand, what you will say, and how to get the best effects in general. Have a clock handy and write in your notebook the number of minutes taken by each demonstration.

Be very critical of yourself. Wherever possible, work in front of a mirror. Have a friend watch you, and invite him to give you his critical reactions. Be open-minded and learn from other people's observations.

Even when practicing, talk in a loud, clear voice full of cheer and confidence. During an actual performance where a microphone is available, try to get a lapel "mike," or one with a neck cord. This allows you more freedom of movement than the one on a stand.

When doing certain demonstrations it is not always necessary to tell the audience what to expect. Also build up a certain amount of suspense by making a few false starts, and working up to a climax. You have seen professionals do this. They have several failures, and then pow! they wind up with a sock finish.

Take pride in your showmanship. Never show anybody anything for which you have to apologize. Nobody is interested in alibis! Practice pays off in smoother performances. But remember too, that the best cure for nervousness is thorough preparation.

17

PROGRAMING

To get the utmost entertainment from your science show, you should start off with a bang. Use an especially good demonstration to capture the interest of your audience, so that more of the same will be expected. Another rule used by expert showmen is to have a brilliant, flashy ending.

Pace your show. Never tire your audience by letting the show lag because of dead spots. The program should not be too long or too short. Always leave the people wishing that you had done more for them. Never lose your audience by giving them more and more of your "precious" material.

Be mindful always of whether your group is made up of young children, older people, or students who may know much science. So use suitable material. Never talk above the level of the people, or use big words which you do not explain. Remember too that young children have a short attention span. This means that they get tired and lose interest quickly.

Your show may be on one topic, or you may mix the themes of your demonstrations. And do not forget to keep a notebook listing your shows. Enter the date, place, and total time. List some of the remarks you made and finally evaluate the show, giving yourself suggestions for future changes.

Adding spice to a science show

PATTER

Patter is the continuous easy line of talk you deliver while demonstrating. A pleasant, humorous flow of bright remarks is sure to add much snap to your show.

Science is fascinating and often so unbelievable that part of your charm will be in explaining it simply and in a light vein. Do not be afraid to make an occasional funny remark which is wild and outlandish. The people will know when you are spoofing them, and they will enjoy it immensely.

However, in a science show you must be very careful to avoid making a humorous and untruthful remark which may be believed by even a few people. Most people know that we are living in a marvelously complicated world, where science can perform wonders. So if you say something funny, make sure that no one will think you are even partly serious.

For example, you may be demonstrating some mysterious effect of magnetism. Suppose you make a joke and say, "This is operated by a radioactive chemical called X-3 phosphorsand." Now this statement is too close to reality. It is amazing how many people will believe you. After all, science is wonderful, especially the chemistry of radioactivity. So maybe there is an X-3 phosphorsand.

A much better funny remark would be, "This is operated by a regiment of specially trained invisible caterpillars." Nobody believes this for a moment, but the hilarious nature of your remark tickles the listeners.

Of course, before your demonstration is over, you must become serious and give the correct scientific explanation. But a good line of humor makes your science lesson more acceptable and enjoyable, and keeps the show alive and sparkling.

Always pause during laughter, so that the audience will hear your following remarks. Remember too that it is good to be funny, but that the humor is not the entire show—it is just used to make the audience more receptive.

Much has been said about the importance of keeping a notebook of your work as an entertainer. One of the most useful sections in your book should be reserved for a large collection of suitable gags and funny bits. You hear these on radio, TV, other science or magic shows, and read them in the newspapers and magazines.

When planning the humor for your next show, it is a good idea to read your notes and select those gags you wish to insert in the right places in your presentation. This is much easier than trying to recall some of "those very funny lines" you once heard or used.

Below are some samples of amusing lines with which to begin your collection. Can you see where each one can be profitably used?

1. A time-tested witty way to open a show is to say, "Today I'd like to show you some unusual things, besides myself."
2. Here is something I learned after twelve years of silent meditation and prayer—and three minutes of practice!
3. Watch my arms. See how my fingers never leave my hands.
4. Here is something I invented when I was three years old.
5. Any child can do this after ten years of practice.
6. I studied this five years in Paris, five years in London, and ten years in Vain.
7. I got this from a little old man on Mars, the last time I visited that planet.
8. When pouring a liquid into a glass, say, "I am going to pour 7,651 drops into this glass. One, two, three, 56, 57, 862, 1,259, 7,509, getting close, 7,649, oops! I poured three drops too many! Oh, my! I'm getting careless!"
9. When something fails, make one of these remarks: "I should have done my homework." "My mother told me there would be days like this." "I really do this better in the dark." "Thank God, I don't have to do this for a living." "As my father's good-natured boss once told him, 'If at first you don't succeed—you're fired!'"
10. Please, no applause. Just throw money!

Get the point? These lines are used for continuity, to

give your show a smooth easy flow as you lead up to the factual, scientific explanation. Some of these facts are given in this book with each demonstration. If more material is needed, look up the topics in science books or encyclopedias.

Use your wonderful imagination. Every performer has his own individual character, style, and personality. Develop the side of you which is most effective. Always smile and behave as though you were enjoying the performance immensely yourself.

This feeling is more contagious than measles!

AUDIENCE PARTICIPATION

Within limits, it is very effective to invite people from the audience to help you. This too can be done in a humorous, friendly manner, which will endear you to everyone.

Do not cause a commotion by taking too long to select one or two eager-beavers from the spectators. Just say that you would like to ask an "inmate" from the audience to help—preferably an unmarried one. As the hands start waving madly, quickly signal one person to come up. As the boy or girl comes forward ask, "Do you have a college degree?" or "Are you willing to help me without pay?"

Of course, these humorous suggestions are given throughout this book in case you feel that you wish to use them. If you are naturally a serious person, or if opportunities do not present themselves, by all means omit the wisecracks. However, most demonstrators have discovered that some degree of humor is necessary to take the stiffness out of an educational experience such as a science show.

Under no conditions must you ever allow your assistant to do anything which might hurt or embarrass him. Audiences resent this. People also like to see you thank the helper most graciously when he is done. It is a good policy to give him some small gift for his assistance, perhaps part of the demonstration. Or you may have on hand inexpensive science toys for this purpose.

Do not get too involved with individuals in the audience. A show is not like a classroom lesson, where time is allowed for many questions and answers, or even for experimentation and exploration.

Instead, a show must have a certain rhythm called "pacing" or "timing." Keep pushing the show forward. Do not allow the audience's attention to wander too long from you or from the action you are performing. It is poor showmanship to have dead spots. You may ask questions and say something witty to the one who knows the answer, but do not wait too long.

Some demonstrators ask questions of no one in particular in the audience. Then after a suitable short interval, when everyone is turning the thought over in his mind, the performer answers the question himself. Once in a while it is a good technique to pretend to hear the correct answer and to repeat it.

Sometimes you may wish to warm up an audience.

There are many gay, short, scientific stunts in which the entire group can be invited to participate while seated. Here are some ideas.

To show how all people are put together joint by joint in almost the same way, ask everybody to try to bite their elbows. Probably no one will be able to do this, but it gives your show a merry touch.

Another test of "intelligence and coordination" is to see if the group can do as you do. Keep the outstretched fingers of your left hand close together with the thumb at right angles. Do the same with your right hand. With both palms facing away from you, place one hand exactly over the other. The thumbs are now on opposite sides.

Now try to twirl the thumbs in small circles like oars, while keeping the four fingers of both hands always closed. All the time one hand must be on top of the other and in contact. As you keep doing this, look around and then point to the one who does it first. Announce him as the winner.

Asking people to repeat long, tongue-twisting chemical words is always fun. Try the insect killer D.D.T. This stands for dichlorodiphenyltrichloroethane. Another lulu of a chemical is tetramethyldiaminotriphenylcarbinol.

Another popular audience stunt is the following optical illusion: Ask the audience to place both their outstretched index fingers together about 12 inches from their eyes. Tell them to keep their eyes constantly on the point where both fingers meet, while moving these fingers toward their eyes. At a certain distance, a frankfurter will appear between the two fingers.

As you know, each eye sees a separate image and the brain fuses the two images into one. But at this close distance the brain cannot fuse the contact point of the fingers into one picture.

Throughout this book you will find many enjoyable audience-participation ideas.

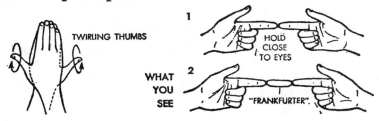

GIMMICK

This is a word used in the entertainment field. It means any hidden or visible device used to help you do something, or get an extra laugh or two.

For example: Display a *large* sign painted, GENIUS AT WORK. Another sign you may show at certain times is, YOU MAY LAUGH NOW. A funny bit is to hold up a sign with the word APPLAUSE on one side. After the audience responds, turn over the sign and it reads, I DESERVE IT.

Another humorous, repeated gag is to have a closed baby-powder can, containing some rice or pebbles. Keep pretending to sprinkle this on things to "make them work." Call it your "special double-duty, up-and-at-em, lollopalooza woofle dust, made from undiscovered prehistoric nanny goats."

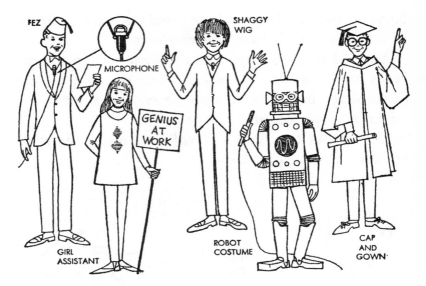

FEZ · MICROPHONE · SHAGGY WIG · GENIUS AT WORK · GIRL ASSISTANT · ROBOT COSTUME · CAP AND GOWN

A gimmick to add color to your demonstrations is the wearing of an easily made, red Turkish fez. Or you might wear a cap-and-gown outfit, used during graduation exercises at high schools and colleges. Then you may be introduced as Dr. Albert Brainstorm, the Mad Professor.

Other devices which will bring smiles to your viewers, include wigs, clown, devil and robot outfits, tuxedos, and imaginative uniforms, such as those of a man from Mars.

Always be on the alert for humorous material. For example, when doing a demonstration involving some form of transportation ask, "Who would like to travel far from here?" When a hand goes up, say, "Here is something to help you along." Then throw the person a road map obtained at a gasoline service station.

A tape recorder, playing a tape of an entire science act, makes a most hilarious gimmick. As you come on the stage, you yawn and stretch. Explain to your audience that you are very tired today, "having worked all night in the hospital performing delicate brain surgery." So you have recorded the entire show, which will be done by some assistants from the audience. They will follow the instructions given by the tape recorder.

Switch on the machine, and set the volume high. Now sit down in a comfortable arm or rocking chair, or lie down on a couch. The recorder plays back your carefully timed, and worded show. Instructions must be crystal clear, and all the apparatus must be foolproof and labeled on the demonstration table.

This can be extremely funny. Questions and explanations must be very critically worded. The tape recorder cracks jokes, gives good-natured scoldings and, in general, behaves like an actual person standing by. Try your hand at this imaginative entertainment gimmick.

A funny gag to close your show with a wild finish is as follows. Say that for your last demonstration you wish to teach something to all the nice people in the audience. Would they like to learn how to agitate billions of air molecules by a novel method involving the laws of motion?

First, hold your handkerchief by one end, with your finger tips. Now ask every person to take out his own clean handkerchief. (This month's, please!) Ask the audience to carefully do exactly as you do.

Use an exaggerated wrist motion to wave the handkerchief up and down, slowly at first, then faster. Finally, when your unsuspecting audience is frantically imitating your waving motion, simply shout, "Bye-bye!, bye-bye! That's all, folks!"—and dash into the wings. If you still have your nerve, come back for a bow!

APPEARANCE OF DEMONSTRATION TABLE

First impressions are very important. Make sure that the audience's first view of your apparatus at the start of the show is exciting. You must give everyone the feeling that "this is going to be interesting."

Whenever possible, try to stand things up for better visibility. Also, have some material such as strings, papers, or wires droop over the front of the table. Have a strong light on everything. Borrow a large colorful tablecloth. Arrange it so that much of the design hangs over the table edge.

However, when demonstrating, it is best to work on a cleared surface. In this way, you focus attention on only what you are doing. An excellent technique is to use one or two tables for displaying the colorful materials until they are needed. These tables may be placed slightly to one side of the stage. The empty demonstration table from which you will work, is then set in the center of the stage.

ELECTRICITY AND MAGNETISM

The obedient puppy

Your reputation is assured, once you demonstrate this unusual homemade toy. The audience sees a small doghouse made from a corrugated paper carton. When you shout, "Come out, Poochy Poo!" a toy puppy mysteriously emerges from the doorway. When you put the animal back into the doghouse, it obediently comes out again and again when you whisper, blow a horn, or even throw a penny at the house!

Instead of a small plastic or wooden dog, you may use a lion, a fire engine, cuckoo, soldier, or anything you wish to work into a very impressive and funny routine. The materials are easily available, and the technical knowledge you will need is very elementary.

The explanation of this novelty is as follows. Inside the doghouse there is a ramp leading down to the door. At the top of this runway is an electromagnet, operated by dry cells which are hidden from view. When the circuit is complete, the magnetism holds the dog, because there is an iron nail or screw attached to its tail end. When the circuit is broken, the dog is released, and gravity pulls it down the steep ramp and out through the door.

On the outside of the doghouse is a large aluminum pie plate, which serves as a circuit breaker. As you see in the illustration, only the upper part of the plate has a screw through it. The springy condition of the rest of the pie plate makes the bottom touch a strip of metal. This contact completes a circuit so that electricity from the dry cells now activates the electromagnet.

Sound waves will shake the pie plate. So will a wind made by blowing. Even throwing a coin at the house will cause a movement which will separate the contacts. Once the circuit is broken, the dog is no longer held by the electromagnet.

You can make the doghouse completely of wood. Then you will have a sturdy, long-lasting device. However, you may find it much easier to use cartons; one carton for the sides, and the corner of another carton for the pitched roof. Masking tape or other adhesives will hold the sections together. If you decide to use cartons, then the rear wall must be made of wood. This wood will hold the electromagnet more securely. The delicate, pie-plate circuit breaker may be mounted on the other side of the board; that is, on the outside rear wall.

In either case, do not forget to provide some available

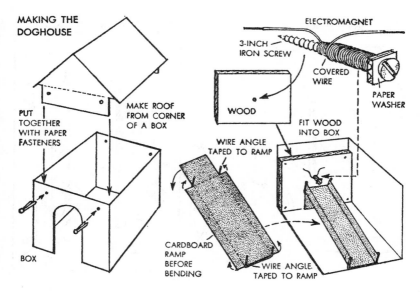

MAKING THE DOGHOUSE

PUT TOGETHER WITH PAPER FASTENERS

MAKE ROOF FROM CORNER OF A BOX

BOX

3-INCH IRON SCREW

ELECTROMAGNET

COVERED WIRE

PAPER WASHER

WOOD

FIT WOOD INTO BOX

WIRE ANGLE TAPED TO RAMP

CARDBOARD RAMP BEFORE BENDING

WIRE ANGLE. TAPED TO RAMP

opening in order to get to the cells, electromagnet, or other parts for servicing. A wooden doghouse may have one of the roof sections hinged. Cartons may have flap hinges. The house may be painted very colorfully, if you wish.

The electromagnet may be obtained from an old broken bell. Carefully draw out some wire from both ends of the bell's electromagnet for your circuit connections. Tie, staple, or use any other means of keeping the electromagnet in the proper position. Another good electromagnet can be made by driving a thick 3-inch *iron* screw into the wooden backboard. Then wind around the screw about 6 to 8 feet of insulated bell wire.

The best electromagnet is made by wrapping about 10 feet of #22 double cotton-covered wire around a 2-inch

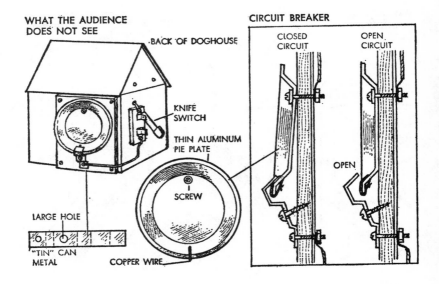

WHAT THE AUDIENCE DOES NOT SEE

·BACK ·OF DOGHOUSE

CIRCUIT BREAKER

CLOSED CIRCUIT

OPEN CIRCUIT

KNIFE SWITCH

THIN ALUMINUM PIE PLATE

SCREW

OPEN

LARGE HOLE

"TIN" CAN METAL

COPPER WIRE

iron wood screw. Cut a small cardboard washer and place it under the head of the screw as shown. This will prevent the end loops of wire from going over the screw head. Drive the screw in at the same slant at which the ramp will be set.

The ramp is cut from corrugated cardboard to give it strength, and bent up to form small guiding walls on its sides. These prevent the dog from falling off the ramp. The walls are kept in this position by clothes-hanger wire, which is bent at right angles. The wire is then taped to the bottom and sides of the ramp. The top lip of cardboard at the start of the ramp is bent over and tacked to the wooden backboard, right under the electromagnet. Position the front end of the ramp so that it leaves the door correctly.

The circuit breaker is a large 12-inch, aluminum pie

plate. Use a screw and washer to fasten it as shown. The open part of the plate should be facing out. By pulling the lower part of the plate toward you, a springy action is obtained. The aluminum should press upward, against a stop made from a strip of sheet metal, carefully cut from a tin can with tin shears or an old pair of large scissors. A good size is 5 inches by 1 inch.

Into the lower end, punch two holes with a sharp nail. These holes are for the screws. The bottom screw tightens the strip into the wood. The upper screw goes through a hole in the strip which is *larger* than the width of the screw. When this screw is tightened or loosened, it adjusts the contact strip against the pie plate.

A copper wire is drawn through the pie plate at the contact point, and tightened down so that it does not move. This makes a more efficient and longer-lasting contact than aluminum.

Connect the circuit as shown. You can see that the electricity must go through the pie plate contacts in order to get to the electromagnet. It is also a good idea to put a knife switch in the circuit, so you can shut off

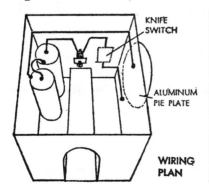

KNIFE
SWITCH

ALUMINUM
PIE PLATE

WIRING
PLAN

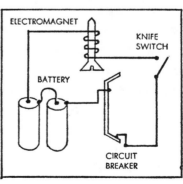

ELECTROMAGNET

KNIFE
SWITCH

BATTERY

CIRCUIT
BREAKER

the current whenever you wish. In this way, you will not have to disconnect your dry cells when the doghouse is not in use.

The best source of electricity is a large (#6) dry cell. Two or more cells will give more positive action. Connect them in series as illustrated.

If you wish, you may place the pie-plate circuit breaker on one side of the house, instead of the rear. Then it may be more convenient to adjust the contacts with one hand, while the other is up front, holding the dog up against the electomagnet.

For best results mount the toy animal on a flat piece of wood which moves easily down the ramp. Better still, you can have the dog roll out quite a distance from the doghouse by attaching small wheels or wooden beads on the wood.

To operate this magnetic doghouse, tighten the contacts on the circuit breaker so that the dog will be held by the electromagnet. Then slowly loosen the adjustment until the circuit is broken and the dog rolls out. Avoid jarring the doghouse. Now tighten the adjustment again, but this time do it very slightly. The device is ready for demonstration.

Place the front of the doghouse at a slight angle to the audience. In this way they can see that there is no contact between you and the house. This also allows room on the table for the dog to roll without falling off the edge. Adjust the reed in a large New Year's party horn so that it makes a very rough sound. Do this by removing the mouthpiece and carefully pulling out the brass

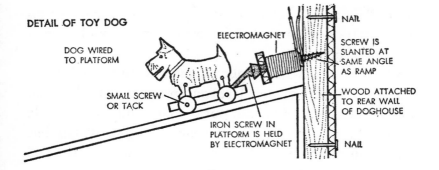

DETAIL OF TOY DOG

DOG WIRED TO PLATFORM

ELECTROMAGNET

SMALL SCREW OR TACK

IRON SCREW IN PLATFORM IS HELD BY ELECTROMAGNET

NAIL

SCREW IS SLANTED AT SAME ANGLE AS RAMP

WOOD ATTACHED TO REAR WALL OF DOGHOUSE

NAIL

reed for a short distance. Direct the sound into the circuit breaker. Call attention to the fact that you are not touching the doghouse. There is only air between the house and you.

Make up a funny story about your dog "Poochy Poo," who comes out when you blow the horn. Say he is hard of hearing, or that he loves parties. That is why you use a horn. Replace the dog after he comes out, and this time shout "Poochy Poo!" into the pie plate. This name has an explosive sound, due to the "poo" sound. Practice saying it loud and almost as if you were blowing out a candle. You might also try using a megaphone, which you can easily make.

The easiest way to get the circuit broken is by blowing. Say that you will blow into your puppy's ear to bring him out. You can use the tightest adjustment on your contacts if you decide to blow. Your audience, of course, thinks that this is the most difficult feat, since the sound is lowest!

Throw a coin against the house. The dog is sure to come out because of the jarring of the contacts. The patter might be that Poochy Poo once belonged to an actor. The dog came out for bows when people threw money on the stage.

You might have a duplicate animal, but very much smaller in size. On your last trial, pretend to replace the dog on the ramp. Instead, put the large dog on one side of the doghouse and put the smaller dog, which has some iron on its back, against the electromagnet. Tell the audience that you once went on vacation, and forgot to leave instructions for feeding the dog. When you came home, you ran to the doghouse and called "Poochy Poo!" At this point, the small duplicate comes out. Pretend that you are heartbroken at seeing your dog so thin and undernourished.

Use your imagination and make up your own act. Explain how this scientific Rube Goldberg contraption works. Many people will not believe that a sane person will go to all this trouble, just to bring a dog out of his doghouse.

Always remember to put the knife switch to the OFF position when you are through. Mark this on your switch. Do not keep the electromagnet activated unnecessarily, because it consumes current rapidly.

Fun with alarm switches

Your audience will think that you are an electrical genius when you show them what marvelous alarms you can design in a moment with just one simple switch.

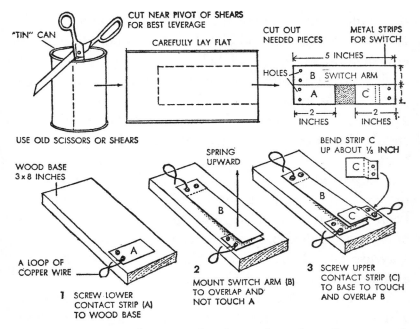

CUT NEAR PIVOT OF SHEARS FOR BEST LEVERAGE

CAREFULLY LAY FLAT

"TIN" CAN

CUT OUT NEEDED PIECES

METAL STRIPS FOR SWITCH

5 INCHES

HOLES

B SWITCH ARM

A

C

2 INCHES

2 INCHES

USE OLD SCISSORS OR SHEARS

WOOD BASE 3 x 8 INCHES

SPRING UPWARD

BEND STRIP C UP ABOUT ⅛ INCH

C

B

A LOOP OF COPPER WIRE

A

1 SCREW LOWER CONTACT STRIP (A) TO WOOD BASE

2 MOUNT SWITCH ARM (B) TO OVERLAP AND NOT TOUCH A

3 SCREW UPPER CONTACT STRIP (C) TO BASE TO TOUCH AND OVERLAP B

You can amuse them with clever burglar alarms and fire warnings. In a jiffy you can change over your act to the production of flood and rain signals, water-level alarms for tanks and swimming pools—and lots more!

The handy, homemade switch is made from 1-inch wide metal. You may obtain this by cutting up tin cans or finding flat steel strips used for heavy crating. Copper bracelet blanks, obtained in arts and crafts shops, are excellent. You will need a 5-inch length for the switch arm, and a pair of 2-inch lengths for the upper and lower contacts. Sandpaper away any lacquer or paint from both ends of each strip, where surfaces will make electrical contact with screws or metal.

Use a nail to punch two holes near the end of each of

the three strips. Screw them down as shown, on a 3-by-8-inch piece of wood about ⅞ inch thick. Loop the end of a 3-inch length of bell wire under one screw of each strip. Of course, a soldered connection would be better. The upper contact should be adjusted so it is about ⅛ inch above the lower contact. The switch arm should be sprung *upward*. See that it makes good contact.

You will also need a loud bell, and one or two large dry cells connected as shown. If you wish, you may keep the cells and bell together on a board or in a container. In order for you to make fast connections, you may use any of the common binding posts or other fast attachments you may be able to obtain.

The best kind is a small (1½-2-inch) alligator test clip, which clamps onto something with a spring action. You can attach a wire to it permanently by simply tightening a screw. Hardware and radio supply stores sell them very inexpensively. If you get eight clips you will be able to make four test wires called "jumpers." Use them for making speedy connections from the bell and cells to the switch.

When presenting your program, have one assistant hold a bell or light, while another holds a dry cell. Show that each item has arrangements for making two attachments. Use jumpers to make the bell or light operate. Explain the meaning of a complete circuit. Remove any wire and show how a circuit is broken.

Make a bell ring and stop by touching the proper wires. Develop the idea of a switch. Tell the audience that people have invented thousands of different switches for all kinds of appliances. Today you are going to explain several interesting alarms.

BURGLAR ALARM

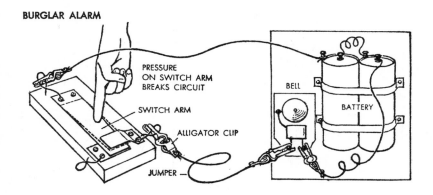

PRESSURE ON SWITCH ARM BREAKS CIRCUIT

SWITCH ARM

ALLIGATOR CLIP

BELL

BATTERY

JUMPER —

Set up the bell circuit so that one switch wire goes to the switch arm and the other to the upper contact. This is a basic alarm circuit. Place a dark cloth, or a handkerchief, over the switch. Now stand an object on the cloth, so that the switch arm is depressed and the circuit broken. Avoid bending down the top contact.

When the object is raised or "stolen," the bell will ring. Use your imagination for different objects your assistants can attempt to "shoplift." Try a vase, supposedly used by the first emperor of China. Another good item is a valise marked, CONTAINS ONE MILLION DOLLARS. You can show that it is overflowing with bills of play money. You might also place a weighted cigar box on the switch, and remark that your father trusts nobody. If you use a candy box, make some humorous remark about your cunning mother.

If you can obtain a battery-operated siren, used on some bicycles, you will add more excitement to your presentation.

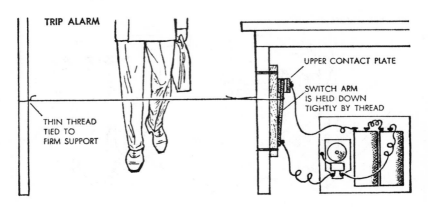

TRIP ALARM

UPPER CONTACT PLATE

SWITCH ARM
IS HELD DOWN
TIGHTLY BY THREAD

THIN THREAD
TIED TO
FIRM SUPPORT

Demonstrate a trip alarm, used in stores and other places to trap prowlers. Attach a thin, *black* cotton thread, a few inches off the floor, to a table or chair.

At the same height and some distance away, carefully lash the ends of your switch to a table leg. Use cord as shown, or small straps. Make a loose loop of the tripping thread around the switch arm, which should be facing the inside of the table. The switch arm should be pressed down when the tripping thread is tight. Hold the loop in place on the switch arm with cellophane tape.

There is another quick way to hold the switch for the tripping alarm. Mount a switch vertically on a plywood base. Then you will have to slip the base under a table leg only, to keep it in place.

Ask an assistant to walk toward you. You can surprise

40

the "prowler" if you have the trap prepared beforehand in an unused part of the stage. If you do not tell the secret first, he will not see the almost invisible black thread. When he walks into the tight thread, it breaks and sets off the alarm.

You might explain that the alarms do not ring bells on the premises only. Private detective agencies and the police often get the signals also.

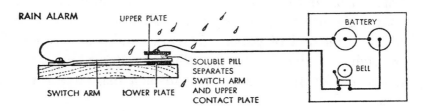

For this, it is most practical to use a rustproof switch made of copper strips. Place a small broken piece of a tablet of Alka-Seltzer or Bromo-Seltzer between the upper contact and the switch arm. A tiny pill of very inexpensive, fast-dissolving saccharin is also good to use.

Place the switch in a large pan and connect your two wires. Sprinkle water from a watering can on the pill, as if it were raining. The wet tablet bubbles and falls apart and the contacts touch, making the bell ring. You might even have a small, battery-operated motor start turning gears which will close a small cardboard window!

This alarm can also be used in basements to warn of leaks and floods.

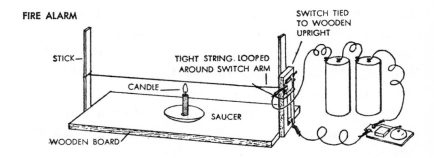

FIRE ALARM

STICK

TIGHT STRING. LOOPED
AROUND SWITCH ARM

CANDLE

SAUCER

WOODEN BOARD

SWITCH TIED
TO WOODEN
UPRIGHT

This is similar to the trip alarm used for burglars. Use your ingenuity to set it up on a smaller scale on a table which is cleared of paper. Place a candle in a saucer and light it under the string. When the string burns, the switch closes the circuit. Instead of a bell have a toy siren go off.

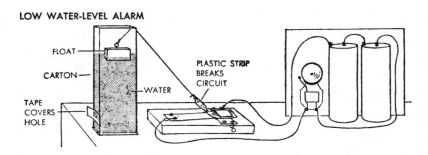

LOW WATER-LEVEL ALARM

FLOAT

CARTON

WATER

PLASTIC STRIP
BREAKS
CIRCUIT

TAPE
COVERS
HOLE

You can show how to make a bell ring when the level in a tank or swimming pool goes down too low.

If you do not have a jar with a faucet near the bottom of it, then you can use a large milk carton. Make a nail hole about 1 inch from the bottom. Cover the hole with cellophane tape, but leave a small tab so you can easily remove the tape later.

Put a nail or screw eye in a block of wood. To this you will attach some cotton thread. This should be long enough to reach the switch contact, when the wood is in the container as it stands next to the switch. At the end of the string leading to the switch, tie a 1-inch-by-2-inch strip of paper, thin plastic, or an old photo negative. This goes between the switch arm and the upper contact.

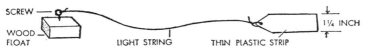

SCREW — WOOD FLOAT — LIGHT STRING — THIN PLASTIC STRIP — 1¼ INCH

Stand the carton near the edge of the table, and next to the narrow side of the switch as shown in the illustration. Fill the container with water, which has had a small amount of milk added to it. This increases the visibility. Use a pitcher when pouring so the audience can really see the liquid entering the container. Place

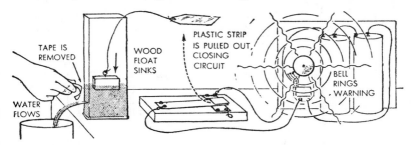

TAPE IS REMOVED — WOOD FLOAT SINKS — PLASTIC STRIP IS PULLED OUT, CLOSING CIRCUIT — BELL RINGS WARNING — WATER FLOWS

the block on the liquid in the carton. Insert the plastic strip where it will break the switch contact.

Get on one side so that everybody gets a good view. Place a large pan a distance below the table and pull the tab from the milk container's nail hole.

As the level goes down, so does the wood. It pulls the

plastic from between the contacts and the alarm goes off. The audience can understand that the same contacts will activate a pump to refill the tank, if the proper arrangements are first made.

If possible, use a tall, clear plastic container instead of the milk carton. Then the lowering of the level will be seen in the container as the liquid streams out. Make the hole with a drill or with the pointed end of sharp scissors.

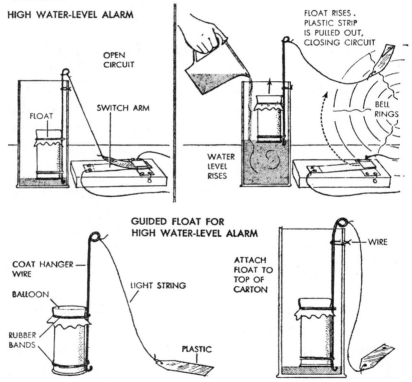

HIGH WATER-LEVEL ALARM

OPEN CIRCUIT

FLOAT

SWITCH ARM

FLOAT RISES. PLASTIC STRIP IS PULLED OUT, CLOSING CIRCUIT

BELL RINGS

WATER LEVEL RISES

GUIDED FLOAT FOR HIGH WATER-LEVEL ALARM

COAT HANGER WIRE

BALLOON

LIGHT STRING

ATTACH FLOAT TO TOP OF CARTON

WIRE

RUBBER BANDS

PLASTIC

This is the same idea, except that a guided float is going to *rise* and pull away the plastic from the contacts. Get a small open can used for frozen orange juice. Tie some thin rubber from a balloon or some plastic around the open top. This is to prevent liquid from dripping into the can when you add some later to the milk carton.

Tie a straight piece of clothes-hanger wire to the can as shown in the illustration. Draw some bell wire or string through two holes in the side of the carton, about an inch from the top. Make a loop here to guide the wire straight up. You may have to put another guide loop about an inch below the top one.

Place the milk carton as you did before, close to the switch. The thread should be *tight*, before you add liquid. As the float rises, it pulls the plastic from the contacts, warning about the danger of overflow.

Here too, a tall, clear plastic container could be used to make the entire operation more apparent to the audience.

CUSTOMER ANNOUNCER

This alarm warns a shopkeeper or home owner that somebody stepped on the alarm switch near the door.

Set up your switch so that you now use only the lower contact and the switch arm. Set the switch on the floor, and place a dark cloth over it. Do not let an assistant

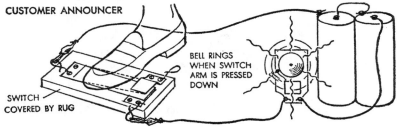

CUSTOMER ANNOUNCER

BELL RINGS
WHEN SWITCH
ARM IS PRESSED
DOWN

SWITCH
COVERED BY RUG

demonstrate this, because he may step on the upper contact and bend it badly. But when you step on the cloth to set off the alarm, step on the part away from the contacts. If you wish, you may mark the cloth above the contacts to guide you.

OTHER ALARMS

Use the switch you made to design an alarm which rings when a baby (doll) is stolen from a crib. Or you may invent a setup where a bell rings when a box is opened. Try to design a device to switch on a circuit when a door is opened.

You can even work up a mind-reading act where a bell mysteriously rings by itself. One ring means "yes," two rings signify "no." The secret is to have the switch set up like a trip alarm. A hidden confederate, or even one out in the open, secretly pulls the invisible thin black thread.

The lighted-bulb puzzle

Show everybody a small electric bulb, half-buried in

sand in a container. The screw-in part of the bulb is up in the air. The light is on, even though there are apparently no electric wires leading to it.

The secret is seen in the illustration. The top screw shell is a dummy, carefully glued on with a clear plastic cement. The bulb beneath it is in a socket. This, and small dry cells, are hidden by the sand.

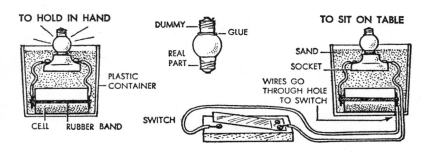

Use round, frosted or painted bulbs, so that the filament cannot be seen. Break one in a cloth, and use pliers to remove any glass chips from the brass screw-in part you need. The setup as shown will make an interesting display.

But if you wish to elaborate and make a bigger trick with this, use a plastic container. Make a hole in the bottom for drawing out the wires to an outside source of current. Place the container on an upturned carton and string two switching wires over the rear edge of a table.

If you spread a large tablecloth to overlap the front of the table you can hide the wires from view all the way down to the floor. Then you may use a foot switch. You can give the audience the impression that the bulb lights

47

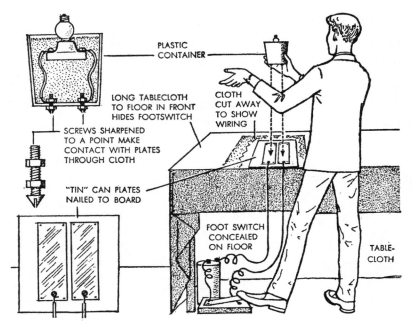

PLASTIC CONTAINER

LONG TABLECLOTH TO FLOOR IN FRONT HIDES FOOTSWITCH

CLOTH CUT AWAY TO SHOW WIRING

SCREWS SHARPENED TO A POINT MAKE CONTACT WITH PLATES THROUGH CLOTH

"TIN" CAN PLATES NAILED TO BOARD

FOOT SWITCH CONCEALED ON FLOOR

TABLE-CLOTH

up only when you touch the bulb with your wand or finger. Say your blood has "charged-up hemogoblins."

The biggest effect is one where you can pick up the entire container away from the table, while the power source and switch are outside. This is done by making the two necessary contacts for the bulb on the bottom of the plastic container with nuts and round-headed bolts. These should be close to the bottom so the container does not stand at a slant.

Confuse everybody by picking up the container, while you hold your fingers over the secret contacts. The light is now off, of course. When you replace the container, you do so on two separated sheets of metal which are flat on the table. These make contact with the bolt-heads.

You can now use your foot switch, and light up the bulb at will.

Furthermore, if the bolts or bolt-heads are sharpened to a point, they can make contact through a loosely woven black cloth hiding the two metal sheets on the table. As you can see, this trick has unlimited possibilities.

Use dry cells or your toy train transformer, and the properly rated bulb for your power source. *Do not use* your house current, unless some responsible adult can make everything thoroughly insulated and foolproof.

AIR PRESSURE

WOODEN BOARD

STRONG PLASTIC BAG

Standing on air

Show a plastic bag as big as a large pillow case. Waft it around so it billows open and fills with air. Then twist the open end closed. Ask what you have inside, and someone is sure to say, "Nothing!" or "It's empty!" If no remarks are forthcoming, pretend that you heard these words said.

Act indignant and say that this so-called emptiness is captured air, which is really stronger than many of us here. Call up a big boy and a small girl. Ask the girl to try to pick you up. Of course, she will find it difficult to do because you are too heavy. Well, since she is having all this trouble, does she think that this bag of air can hold you up? Now ask the audience whether they believe that this feat is possible. There is only one way to find out. Let's try it!

If necessary, refill the bag as before, and close it by twisting the open end many times. Quickly wrap some string securely around the twists, and tie a bowknot. Instruct the girl to put the bag on the floor, and lay a large flat, wooden board on it.

Now pretend to be afraid to stand on the board. Place one foot on, take it off, and put the other one on and off, to build up suspense. After a while, carefully stand on the board with both feet, using the boy for gentle support. Everyone is surprised to see that the air will support your weight.

Explain that this is not so amazing, because out on the street one can see 10,000-pound trucks being supported on air. Of course, the heavy rubber tires can stand the air pressure.

Tell the audience another secret of how you fooled them. When you put the large board over the comparatively weak plastic bag, your weight was spread over a large surface. That means that each square inch on the bag has to support only a small part of your total weight.

Again fill the bag with air. Twist the open end and hold this tightly in your hand. Place it on the floor and ask the boy if he has enough confidence to sit on the bag.

After all, he need not worry, since he would be putting a large sitting surface on the bag to spread the weight!

As the boy sits down carefully, ask him what is holding him up. Then say, "What will happen if I release the air?" Before he can give an answer, let the bag untwist in your hand. The boy will come down to the floor. He will do this safely and slowly, but in a most unbalanced manner, since his legs will be sprawled out.

While the audience is howling, shake the boy's hand and wait for quiet. Congratulate the boy for being such a good sport, and for helping everybody learn that the air around us, though invisible, is a real substance.

The best bag to use is one made of the heavier grade of plastic. Get the largest size you can. There are some about 20 inches wide and 30 inches long, or even larger. Look around for them. They are used by some diaper-service companies and many other businesses. Twenty-five pound boxes of detergent are lined with strong plastic bags. Do a little detective work, and you will find these bags being used somewhere.

If you can obtain only the small sizes you see daily, then you must use lighter objects or smaller boys and girls. The bags must be free from holes. Have several handy at your shows, in case of rare blowouts.

Strong repairs can be made on the spot by using cellophane tape. Some tapes work better on different plastics, so test each type first. If a seam splits in the bag, first roll the plastic together, before putting on the tape.

An interesting bit of byplay is to do something with the air escaping from the bag as you squeeze it. Hold the open end so the air comes out in a small stream. Make this wind blow your assistant's hair. Or have a propeller turn. You might also put the end over the blowing part of a whistle or a toy horn. Experiment to find the best location to place the bag on a flute, recorder, or slide whistle, so that you can play it like a bagpipe. The hole in the mouthpiece must *not* be covered.

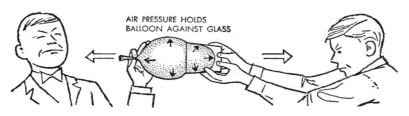

AIR PRESSURE HOLDS
BALLOON AGAINST GLASS

Use this act to demonstrate other ways air does work for us. For example, blow up a balloon while it is in a glass or a deep cup. While you hold the inflated balloon by the twisted neck, pick up the container. Ask your assistants to try to pull the cup away from the balloon which you are holding. It is not easily done. Make it seem harder by slightly moving your arm toward them as they pull. Make the point that the air is pressing the rubber against the cup.

Incidentally, a *large* heavy rubber balloon will also support a person when a large flat board is laid over it first.

The weightless milk mystery

Let us take a well-known air-pressure demonstration and

see how it can be presented with a new slant, full of mystery and showmanship.

No doubt you have seen the stunt where a drinking glass is filled with water from a pitcher, and a cardboard is placed over the top. Then the glass and the cardboard are both slowly turned over while they are being held. When the hand is removed from the cardboard, the paper remains in place under the glass, even though the water inside seems to be pressing down on it.

The scientific explanation is that air pressure does not only act downward, but also sideways and even upward. It is this upward pressure which is holding up the cardboard, as well as the water on top of it.

The method described above is how this demonstration is usually done, even on a science show. Now we shall present a dramatic improvement.

A boy and a girl come on stage. The boy does the water and cardboard trick in the same manner described above. One difference, however, is that instead of water he uses a white liquid, made by adding a small amount of milk to the water. This improves the visibility. Also, while he is holding the overturned glass with the water and cardboard over a basin, he asks the girl if she is brave enough to put her head under the glass. She does this like a heroine, much to the delight of the audience, which is shouting, "No, No, No!" and "Go ahead!"

After the act, the boy explains the science principle. Then he sticks his thumbs under his armpits and struts around the stage, pretending to be very proud of himself.

MILKY WATER

The girl shakes her head in disgust at the boy's peacock display of vanity. She shakes her finger under his nose and says, "Now you watch me!" She repeats his trick in every respect. While she is holding the overturned glass, the boy indicates that this is exactly what *he* did. So what is she crowing about?

At this point, the girl holds up a finger and says, "Watch this." She then peels away the paper—*and the liquid still remains in the overturned glass!* The boy pretends to recoil in exaggerated astonishment. The audience gasps, and then remains remarkably quiet, trying to figure this out.

The girl asks the audience to count aloud together to ten, and then blow toward the stage. The liquid will then obediently leave the glass. The gleeful spectators help out as requested, while the girl says, "Please don't blow me off the stage!" Then, wonder of wonders, the liquid spills into the basin as the girl predicted. The girl now picks up a large picket sign which reads, GIRLS ARE SMARTER THAN BOYS. For a few seconds she struts as the boy did before. Then she walks over to him while he pretends to behave like a beaten dog, and puts out her hand in friendship. He shakes it, and she holds up her

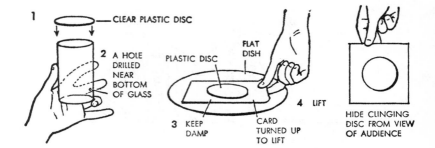

1 — CLEAR PLASTIC DISC

2 A HOLE DRILLED NEAR BOTTOM OF GLASS

PLASTIC DISC

FLAT DISH

4 LIFT

3 KEEP DAMP

CARD TURNED UP TO LIFT

HIDE CLINGING DISC FROM VIEW OF AUDIENCE

hand to get absolute quiet from the audience. She then explains how she fooled everybody.

When she picked up the cardboard, a circular piece of plastic was stuck to it. When she placed the cardboard on the glass of water, she was gently positioning the plastic over the top of the rim.

Then she held the cardboard carefully, with the plastic under it, against the glass as she turned the setup over. When she *slowly* peeled away the cardboard, she was extremely careful not to disturb the plastic.

This was invisible, and made the entire affair most illogical and mysterious. In order to release the plastic, she removed her finger from a small hole, which had been drilled in the glass about ½ inch from the bottom. Before the hole was uncovered, air pressure from below held up the liquid. When the finger was removed, air came into the glass. Then the air pressure on top of the liquid was the same as the air pressure below it, so gravity pulled out the liquid. The clear plastic fell unnoticed with the water into the basin.

The ⅛-inch hole in the glass can be drilled for a few cents by a professional glazier, who has special drills.

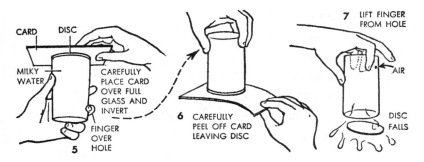

CARD DISC

MILKY WATER

CAREFULLY PLACE CARD OVER FULL GLASS AND INVERT

FINGER OVER HOLE

5

6 CAREFULLY PEEL OFF CARD LEAVING DISC

7 LIFT FINGER FROM HOLE

AIR

DISC FALLS

Or you can use a clear plastic glass, sold everywhere for a dime, and drill your own hole. An easy way to make a hole is to stick a red-hot, small nail or needle into the plastic glass. Hold the nail with pliers while heating over the gas-range flame. However, a drill makes a cleaner hole. So does the point of small sharp scissors.

If you do not wish to make a hole, you may release the plastic by flipping it with your small finger while holding the glass. The motion will be unnoticed.

The plastic must be thin, stiff, clear, and not warped. Cut a suitable piece from some plastic box or from other discarded, flat plastic items. The best cardboard to use is a square piece cut from a postal card. Then you can "peel" it away more easily from the plastic, which is held under the glass by a very weak force. It takes a few tests beforehand to learn the knack. Practice over the sink.

Before the show, wet the cardboard and press the plastic circle against it. You will find that now you can pick up the paper and that the plastic will adhere to it.

Place the moist paper on a flat plate, with the plastic facing up. Put some obstruction in front of the plate so the audience cannot get a glimpse of the plastic. Press the plastic against the center of the paper. Do not keep the paper soaked. At the same time, never allow it to dry, or the plastic will not stick to it.

Have one corner of the paper slightly curled, so you can pick it up more easily. You should be able to hold the paper vertically, without losing the plastic. The plastic should be facing you, and not the audience.

Guns apoppin'

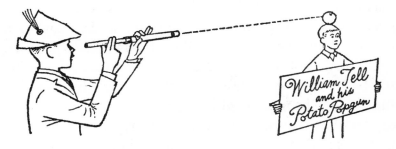

Many thousands of years ago, the brilliant idea of making a popgun toy probably entered the playful mind of a caveman with an exceptionally high intelligence. All this clever fellow needed were some slices of potatoes, and some kind of smooth, hollow tube made from sugar cane or from other natural sources.

Today in our wonderful technical world there are dozens of tubes you can choose. They are made of plastic, metal, glass, fiber, or wood.

The simple technique has not changed throughout the years. Cut ¼- to ½-inch slices of raw potatoes, and

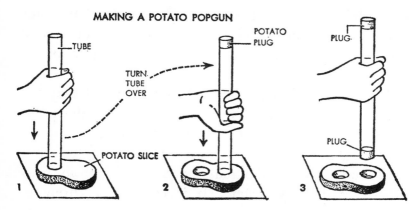

MAKING A POTATO POPGUN

TUBE

TURN. TUBE OVER

POTATO PLUG

PLUG·

PLUG.

POTATO SLICE

1   2   3

place them on a flat plate. Using a twisting motion, press the end of the tube on a slice. An airtight plug is cut, and inserts itself into the tube.

Turn the tube over and put a plug into this end also. Use a dowel stick slightly smaller than the tube as a pusher, and move one plug toward the other. The moving plug compresses the air molecules before it. These behave like a spring.

Soon the air pressure becomes strong enough to overcome the friction of the plug against the side of the tube. With a sudden release, the plug shoots forward. The popping sound is made as the strong air waves,

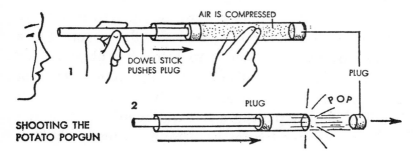

AIR IS COMPRESSED

DOWEL STICK PUSHES PLUG

PLUG

1

2   PLUG   POP

PLUG

SHOOTING THE POTATO POPGUN

which are produced, strike your ear drums. The faster you move the pusher, the greater is the compression. The plug goes farther and faster, and the pop is louder too.

The slices are more easily cut by the tube if they are on some cardboard or felt. No need to squander potatoes, for a plug bullet, if it is not mutilated, can be reused many times.

A handy, glass tube may be borrowed from your father's car-battery tester. It is called a hydrometer and looks like a large medicine dropper. You will have to remove the rubber bulb and spout.

Instead of using the second potato plug with its pusher, you can make an effective piston as follows. Get a dowel stick (round wooden rod) which is slightly smaller than the tube. Wind thin cotton thread around one end, so that it forms a tight-fitting piston washer. Let it soak in water and it will swell and become airtight.

Use many kinds of homemade potato guns when explaining the science principles involved. Then stand up little wooden figures and try to hit them down. For visibility, get down low and closer to the audience, even offstage if necessary. Shoot toward the stage so everybody can see the person shooting, and also the target. Place empty cartons as backstops to catch the plug bullets.

You will have no difficulty getting contestants from the audience. You may also do a funny, harmless William Tell act, by placing a red cardboard apple on the head of a cooperative assistant and trying to shoot it down. The person balancing the apple should have his back to William Tell. Think of other ways of entertaining with these potato guns. How about having a western "fast-draw act" between a gunman and sheriff?

Show and operate a factory-made popgun. Explain how the cork pops when the trigger releases a spring. This sends a plunger down the barrel, compresses the air, and fires the cork bullet.

If you wish, you may explain that real guns and cannons operate on the same principle. However, in real guns the compression is caused by the sudden release of tremendous volumes of expanded gases from gunpowder.

You can make a smaller, "pea shooter" type of potato gun by using a plastic drinking straw. Find the widest drinking tube and use a thin wooden applicator as a pusher. The plugs are tiny and cannot easily be used again. Try this out of doors because the small plugs are not easily found. If shot indoors, they might be difficult to clean up after some target practice.

Invisible giant crushes a can

Audiences always love to see one of the gigantic and unbelievable forces of nature go through its paces— even if they have seen it before.

Air may not be visible, but it surely is around us. Since air is a mixture of gases which have weight, it

presses on things. And since air extends upward for hundreds of miles, this squeezing effect can be very powerful. In fact, at sea level every square inch of any surface has 15 pounds pressing on it in all directions.

Show an empty 1-, 2-, or 5-gallon metal can. There are hundreds of square inches of surface on it. Why then does it not collapse from all the air pressure on the outside? Because there is air inside under the same pressure. That means each square inch of can surface is being pushed on both sides by the same force.

What would happen if most of the air were removed from the inside? Many hundreds of pounds of air would now be pressing on the outside surface of the can, and not being pushed back from the inside. Will the steel can be able to stand this tremendous extra outside force without folding up? Let's see.

It is too bad that we do not usually have an exhaust pump which takes air out of a container. But we have a good scheme for driving out the air in another way. Pour a glass of water into the can. Leave the cover off, and place the can on an electric stove or hot plate so the water inside will boil. Let it steam strongly for five minutes or more. Since steam vapor is really greatly expanded water, it is driving out the air.

Finally, shut off the heat. Use a cloth to lift the can by its handle onto a baking pan resting upside down on a pad of newspapers. This is done to prevent damage to the table surface. Quickly screw on the cover tightly. This must have its usual airtight fiber washer, so that no air can get in.

As the steam cools and condenses back to water, it shrinks. Since no air can now enter the closed can, the pressure inside is much less than outside. The "invisible giant of air pressure" now exerts its mighty squeeze. In a few minutes the can looks as though an elephant had stepped on it. If you are using a microphone, place it near the collapsing can. It is fun to hear the steel being bent.

To hasten the condensation of the steam you may sprinkle cold water on the can. If you have a similar uncollapsed can, hold it next to the one you used. It makes a dramatic comparison.

The can must be washed with a detergent before use. Get rid of any oil, explosive materials such as gasoline or paint solvents. There must be no cracks or open seams in the can.

Use a good hot plate. However, since it often takes a little time to boil the water, have an assistant keep the steaming can ready for you. This might be done on the side of the stage.

If you are all alone, or if you are starting with cold water, then you may wish to do another demonstration while the air is being steamed out of the can.

MOTION

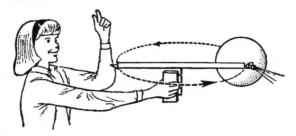

Rocket merry-go-round

The audience will thoroughly enjoy the motion, color, and variety of your homemade merry-go-round, powered by air-filled balloons. While in this mood, they will listen intently to any interesting facts you may tell them about jets, rockets, and space satellites.

If you blow up a balloon and let it go, it scoots all over the place. But you will always notice that as the air goes out in one direction, the balloon moves in the opposite direction. More than 200 years ago a famous scientist, Sir Isaac Newton, stated that for every force acting in one direction, there is an equal force acting in the opposite direction. This is called "reaction."

In a balloon, jet-propelled airplane or rocket, there is a mass of gas sent backward with some considerable force. But this gas exerts an exactly equal and opposite force on the container. The reaction drives the balloon, jet, or rocket forward. Reaction takes place even when there is no outside air. That is why rockets can operate up in space, which is mainly a vacuum.

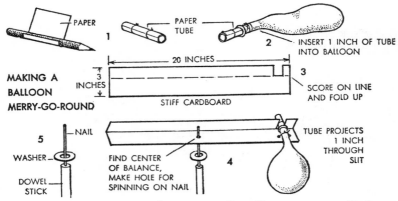

PAPER

PAPER TUBE

1

2 — INSERT 1 INCH OF TUBE INTO BALLOON

MAKING A BALLOON MERRY-GO-ROUND

3 INCHES

20 INCHES

STIFF CARDBOARD

3

SCORE ON LINE AND FOLD UP

5

NAIL

WASHER

DOWEL STICK

FIND CENTER OF BALANCE, MAKE HOLE FOR SPINNING ON NAIL

4

TUBE PROJECTS 1 INCH THROUGH SLIT

The merry-go-round seen in the illustration will demonstrate the force of reaction and will also guide your balloons in a circular path. You may use large round balloons, or the long sausage types.

First, make a 3-inch-long tube by rolling a 3-by-6-inch piece of light cardboard around a pencil. An old postal card is excellent. Use string or cellophane tape to prevent the tube from unraveling. Insert about 1 inch of the tube into the neck of the balloon. Wrap light string around the rubber to hold the tube securely in position.

Next get a very stiff piece of cardboard 3 inches by 20 inches. Old window-display signs at your drug store are perfect. To give the strip extra stiffness, bend up at right angles, 1 inch of the long side. To get a smooth even bend, first score the bending line with a sharp pencil or other pointed object. Fold the cardboard *away* from this slightly cut line.

Cut a small slit in the bent-up part, about 1 inch from one end. Lay the balloon down so that the paper tube projects through this slit for about 1 inch. Pierce two tiny holes into the cardboard. Then draw some string

66

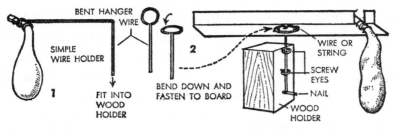

through them or twist some wire to hold the tube in the position shown in the illustration.

The entire strip should now be balanced over a finger, in order to find the place around which the merry-go-round will rotate on a nail. The hole in the cardboard should be round and slightly larger than the nail. Drive the nail into the end of a long stick. Or you may drill a hole and insert a long, but slightly thinner nail in it. Put washers around the nail under the cardboard. This cuts down the friction.

A better and smoother-turning shaft is made from a length of clothes-hanger wire. Bend a loop in the wire at right angles. Secure the loop to the top of the cardboard with wire or string as shown. Some string is wound around the metal shaft just as it comes out of the bottom of the cardboard. The shaft is now securely held in the proper position. It may be inserted into a vertical hole drilled into the end of a stick. The shaft must move freely and stick out far enough, so the merry-go-round does not touch the top of the wood.

Better than a hole in the wood is a bearing made by screwing three small screw eyes in a vertical line near the top of the post. The wire shaft is inserted into the carefully placed openings of the screw eyes. It is prevented from going down too far by a nail, driven on the vertical line a short distance under the bottom screw eye. Smooth away burrs and make sure the shaft is straight. Adjust the merry-go-round so that when it swings it does not always stop in the same place.

When blowing up the balloon, place your finger over the end of the tube between breaths. This prevents escape of air. With a properly inflated balloon, you should be able to get at least ten merry-go-round turns. Have some spares for an important show.

For greater variety you may make whirligigs with two differently colored balloons, mounted at each end of the strip and facing opposite the other. Another style is made completely from bent clothes-hanger wire. Follow the bends in the illustration.

The wooden posts *must be held vertically* by your assistant. A better way might be to tie the post in the proper vertical position to a table or chair.

If you want the rocket balloons to travel in a straight direction, stretch some copper wire or string tightly between two objects or assistants. Place a soda straw on the wire and attach the balloon to it by means of cellophane tape as shown. Attach the tape while the balloon is inflated. A little practice will teach you the best method of doing this.

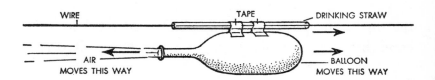

And away we go!

All you need is a small cart, either bought or homemade, and you are ready for the demonstrations. With a few more small items you can present a complete act on the laws of motion, safety, friction, and why a ramp makes work easier.

Look in some child's toy chest for a light cart with wheels. If you cannot obtain this, you can easily build the attention-getting colorful one described below.

You will need a board 13 inches long, no less than 7 inches wide, and ¾ of an inch thick. To this you will attach four small wheels you may have in the house. Or you may use four similar screw-on covers from large jars. The colors may be different.

Pierce an axle hole in each cover with an awl or a

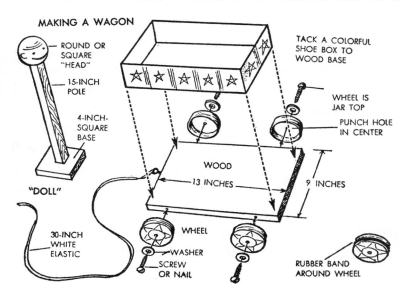

MAKING A WAGON

ROUND OR SQUARE "HEAD"

15-INCH POLE

4-INCH-SQUARE BASE

"DOLL"

30-INCH WHITE ELASTIC

TACK A COLORFUL SHOE BOX TO WOOD BASE

WHEEL IS JAR TOP

PUNCH HOLE IN CENTER

WOOD

13 INCHES

9 INCHES

WHEEL

WASHER

SCREW OR NAIL

RUBBER BAND AROUND WHEEL

sharp nail. To get the exact center, make a circular tracing of the top of the cover on a sheet of paper. Carefully cut out the circle and fold it exactly in half. Now again fold the paper in half. Open the paper and set it evenly over the top of the cover. Pierce the metal where the two creases cross. The burr raised in the metal is now on the inside and should not affect the smooth operation of the "wheel."

The nail used for piercing should not be much larger than the screw you will use to attach the covers to the wood. Place washers under the screws. Flat-headed nails may also be used as axles. These should be in the middle of the thickness of your wood, and at right angles. Go in far enough from the front and back ends of the board, so that the wheels are entirely propped against the wood.

If you worked carefully, all four wheels should be touching the floor at the same time. The wheels *must be loose.* Do not worry about their wobbling. To get traction on the smooth floor, put flat rubber bands around each wheel. The wheel which is not touching the floor may often be built up by several layers of rubber bands.

Find a sturdy, colorful shoe box and tack it, open end up, to the wood as shown. *Save the box cover;* you will need it for a demonstration later. Place a screw eye in one end of the board. Attach to it a 30-inch length of ¼-inch *white* elastic. Wider elastic is more visible, of course. Try some, but it must stretch easily.

In your demonstrations you will need something to act

as your "standing passenger." You may use a large 15-inch rigid doll. Attach the bottom of the figure on the center of a 4-inch square, thin plywood or heavy corrugated cardboard. If no doll is available, use a 15-inch-long wooden pole, at least 1½ inches square. You may wish to put a colorful doll's head on it. Perhaps you can attach a square block for a head, or just paint facial features on the pole. Remember that color always increases showmanship.

Here are some demonstrations you can perform with this apparatus.

INERTIA OF REST

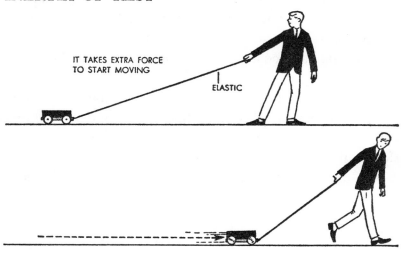

IT TAKES EXTRA FORCE
TO START MOVING

ELASTIC

An object at rest will remain in that position unless some force moves it. In fact, there is a tendency to resist being moved. This is called "inertia." This is why cars start slowly and must use special gears to relieve the strain on the engine. When starting a vehicle, an extra amount of force is needed to overcome inertia of rest.

You can show this by placing the empty cart on the floor. Now prepare to pull it by holding the elastic to its full, unstretched length. Pull the cart rather quickly and walk across the stage. The stretch is greatest for a second or two as the cart gets started. Then when it is under way, the pulling stretch visibly becomes less.

Now stand the figure in the *front* part of the shoe box and quickly pull the elastic forward. The cart goes forward, but the "passenger" falls backward. This is what occurs in a bus. The engine pulls the car forward, but if this is done fast, then the person's inertia keeps him in the same spot for an instant. Since a person is not built rigidly, and he is also not attached to the floor with bolts, he loses his balance and moves backward. The heads of sitting passengers also bob back on starting.

Show that if you start the cart *slowly,* the elastic will not stretch very much. Also, that the passenger will not fall, if a car is started slowly. A good driver starts slowly, in order to overcome the car's inertia.

Again stand the passenger in the front part of the box.

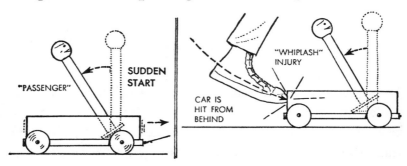

Pretend that another automobile whacks the rear of the cart. Do this by kicking forward the back end of your cart. The figure again goes back. If a person were sitting, his head would bob back very fast. He might get a neck injury called a "whiplash." Astronauts and pilots of fast jet planes have padded head rests, because their vehicles gather speed so suddenly.

INERTIA OF MOTION

Objects in motion tend to continue in motion and in a straight line, unless stopped by some force. The resistance to change of motion is also called inertia.

Place the figure near the *back* of the shoe box. Start off slowly so that the passenger does not fall. When the cart has sufficient speed, have it bump against a chair, foot, or another car.

The figure falls forward, because its inertia tends to make it continue moving forward. The car too had inertia, but it was stopped suddenly by a strong force. Explain why people in auto accidents often go through

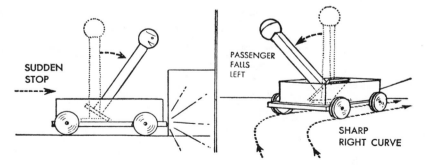

SUDDEN
STOP

PASSENGER
FALLS
LEFT

SHARP
RIGHT CURVE

windshields. Why are seat-belts important? How many in the audience have seat-belts? Why do heads bob forward when a bus slows down or stops?

Now show how inertia makes our bodies swerve when a car goes around a curve. Place the figure in the middle of the box. Move the cart forward in a straight line. Build up speed, and then make a quick right turn with the cart. The figure's inertia tends to make it continue in a straight line. It falls to the *left* because the car has moved to the *right*.

Make left turns with the cart, to show how people in buses will move to the right. Explain why cars must go slowly around curves to avoid going off the road. If roads are slanted or banked correctly, the cars are helped to make safe turns. A slant for a left turn has the left side of the road lower. Gravity pulls the left side of the car down and to the left. This force works against the car's tendency to move to the right.

REACTION

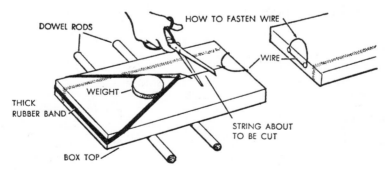

DOWEL RODS
HOW TO FASTEN WIRE
WIRE
WEIGHT
THICK RUBBER BAND
STRING ABOUT TO BE CUT
BOX TOP

On page 65 you learned about this law of motion as you

74

demonstrated rockets. Now you can show reaction at work in another way, by using the cover of the shoe box which you saved.

Set the box cover upright upon two or three dowel sticks (around flag sticks), so it can easily roll over them. Place a section of a heavy rubber band around the front end of the box cover, as shown in the illustration. Stretch the rubber band toward the rear like a sling-shot. Tie it with light string to a wire loop anchored in the rear of the cardboard cover.

Place a small but heavy weight (about one pound) in the rubber sling. When you dramatically cut the string with scissors, the weight shoots forward for a few feet. The box cover zooms away in the opposite direction. This shows Newton's law of reaction at work. To every action there is an equal and opposite reaction.

Read any science book for many more examples of inertia and reaction which you can demonstrate. Tell your story in an interesting manner.

Making work easier

There are many more uses for the shoebox cart. If you wish to lengthen your act with it, you can demonstrate how much easier it is to roll things, rather than to slide them. You may also show that it is easier to move the cart up a slant to an elevated place, than lift it up to that location.

ROLLING AND SLIDING FRICTION

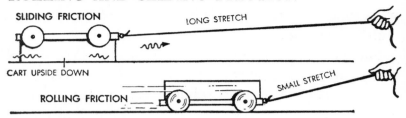

Reverse the cart so that the box is on the floor with the wheels up in the air. Hold the elastic and pull the cart in this position. The stretch will be very long. Turn the cart back on its wheels and measure the pulling force now needed. The stretch is much less.

Explain why sliding friction is greater than rolling friction. If you wish, you may explain how primitive man used to drag objects. Then the wheel was invented and revolutionized the carting of heavy objects.

You may also bring into your demonstration other ways of reducing friction. Point out that sometimes we even increase friction, if we find it useful.

RAMPS

You can use the stretch of the elastic to show how work can be made easier because of a slanted road.

Pick up the cart by the elastic and let it dangle in the air. The stretch, of course, is tremendous. You may have to stand on a stool. Explain that this stretch is a measure of the force you would need to lift the cart ver-

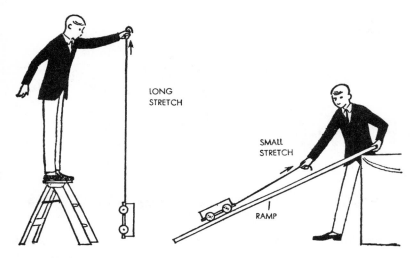

LONG STRETCH

SMALL STRETCH

RAMP

tically up to the table. You may record the stretch by means of a ruler, string, or by marking a long stick.

Now get a long plank which can be slanted from the floor to the top of the table. Pull the cart up this ramp. The elastic stretches much less. If you cannot get a plank, then move the cart on a table which is slanted.

Explain that the work is made easier and more convenient by a ramp. However, you must point out that the distance covered is much greater when a slanted road is used. Discuss why roads wind around mountains, and why we have stairs instead of ropes or ladders in our homes.

BALANCE

Mystery of the balancing butterflies

Everybody will wonder what you are going to do when you show them the large cardboard model of a beautifully colored butterfly. Then you place the head of the butterfly on the tip of your finger, and it clings to it horizontally, defying all logical notions of balance.

Lay the head and wing tips over the edge of a table. The side view shows almost all of the butterfly's body hanging unsupported. Next put the point of a sharpened pencil, or a long stick with a nail in the end, under the insect's head.

The butterfly remains balanced and horizontal—even if you spin it, or move the support in many unvertical directions! You may show many more colorful butterfly models, and also birds, dragonflies, or airplanes. Invite half a dozen people to help you display these perplexing toys. The motion, color, and mystery will enhance your show tremendously.

There are two reasons the butterfly remains balanced so securely. First, there are pennies, iron washers, or even small sheets of lead taped to the cardboard. These are placed so that their weight balances the rest of the paper butterfly on the other side of the pivot.

Secondly, the cardboard has been ruled and scored down the middle, from head to rear. The weights on each wing pull the cardboard down. Most of the weight of the model is now *below* the pivot support. This is the scientific reason for stability. As you well know, it is more difficult to tip over something which is heavier lower down than on top.

To cut the models shown in the illustrations, get some graph paper or rule your own lines. Copy each outline on your larger graph exactly as it is shown on the small graph lines. You may make your model any size, of course, by giving different values to your line spaces.

Use a stiff cardboard, but the lightest which will do the job. If the weights make the wings sag too much, your paper is probably too thin. You may tape a folded strip of cardboard across, from wing to wing, for extra support. Or you may use a thin, flat strip of wood found in kindergartens for making fans, etc. A wooden medicinal applicator is also good.

Use cellophane tape to place the weights *as far forward* as possible. If the weights are not sufficient, use more. It is very spectacular if you get the pivot as far as possible toward the end of the model. The weights may be hidden from view. Cover them with a similar sheet of cardboard, carefully taped or glued at the seams. If you paint designs over the butterfly, you can add to the illusion.

Do not make a hole for the pivot. You will get more swaying if you only make a dimpled depression. Now that you know the idea behind this toy, design and modify your own models. Ask your spectators to do the same.

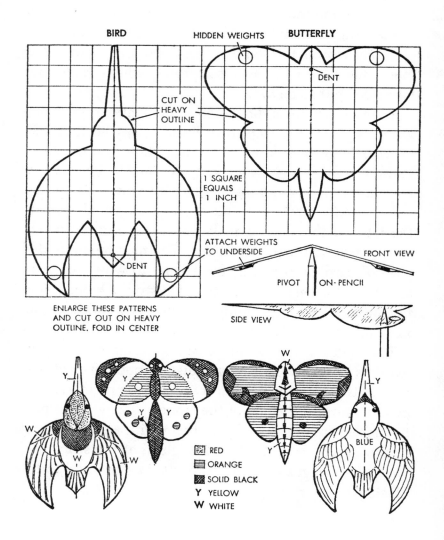

Unusual way to find balancing point

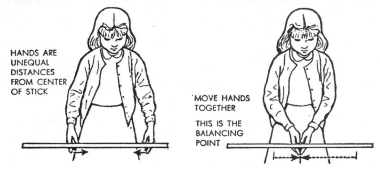

HANDS ARE UNEQUAL DISTANCES FROM CENTER OF STICK

MOVE HANDS TOGETHER

THIS IS THE BALANCING POINT

On the stage there are many lengths of sticks; rulers, yardsticks, window poles, odd-shaped rods, and a baseball bat. You declare that you can find the balancing point by a scientific stunt. You do this by placing one finger of each hand beneath each end of the horizontally held stick, and then slowly drawing your fingers together.

No matter where you place your fingers under a ruler, or any regularly shaped object, they will meet at the middle. If the object is of irregular shape, your fingers will meet at the balancing point, which may not be in the middle. Have assistants do this on various sticks and they will get the same results. Try it on a baseball bat. The place where the balancing occurs in all of these items contains the "center of gravity." This is where all the weight of the object seems to be concentrated.

Place one finger at about the 7-inch mark on a 12-inch ruler. The other should be at about 1 inch. Start moving the fingers together slowly, and only the finger at the 1-inch mark will move until it gets close to the middle.

The explanation has to do with the weight and the

friction of the object against your finger. The greater the weight, the greater the friction. And as friction increases, there is less sliding. So, if one finger moves a short distance ahead of the other one, the weight of the stick on that finger increases and sliding slows up or stops.

Find many long, but narrow objects, both regularly shaped or heavier or larger at one end. For example, a broom, mop, or wooden cooking spoon, make excellent demonstration materials.

You can also improve this act by showing that the center of gravity, or balancing point, of a bat is *not* the best spot to hit a baseball. First find the balancing point of a bat. Mark it by tying a narrow red ribbon around the spot.

Now hold the bat handle loosely between the thumb and forefinger. Have an assistant strike the bat sharply at different places, up and down. Use a rubber mallet, or a cloth-covered hammer. At one point the audience will hear a sound which is most solid. You will also feel the least vibration. Put a white ribbon around this spot. This is what players call the "sweet spot." There is less danger of splitting, if the bat strikes the ball here.

The place is not called the center of gravity, but instead, it is the center of percussion. It is usually between 2 and 10 inches from the thick end of the bat. If the ball is struck above or below this point, the bat tries to swing around this point. This twisting force tries to wrench the bat out of the hands and makes the bat sting. In a "handle hit," the bat may even split.

More balancing stunts

Place one end of a ruler over the end of a table or chair, and it will fall off. Yet when you attach a heavy hammer to the overhanging ruler, it will now rest perfectly still in this most illogical position.

The hammer is looped under the ruler by a piece of string, as shown in the illustration. The heavy metal head is now *under* the point of support of the ruler. Because the center of gravity of the ruler-and-hammer combination is in this position, the balance is very stable.

Just for fun, after your explanation you can place a wand over the table edge. But this time it will remain in this position—even without a hammer under it! The reason is that the wand is a hollow paper tube. Inside, there are one or two 1-ounce lead fishing weights. You can slide these from end to end to confuse people.

Make such a wand by wrapping paper around a ⅞-inch dowel stick. Glue the inside edge to the first turn, so you have a clear cylinder inside. Use tape, glue, or gum paper for the outside surface. If the lead weights are too tight and will not slide, hammer them narrower. Glue corks or dowel pieces in the ends. Paint the wand black. You might also use a long mailing tube, and a large 6-ounce lead fishing sinker. Glue corks flush inside the ends of the tube.

Another spectacular balancing trick, is to try to balance the side of a glass milk bottle across a string, stretched between two assistants. This can be done by

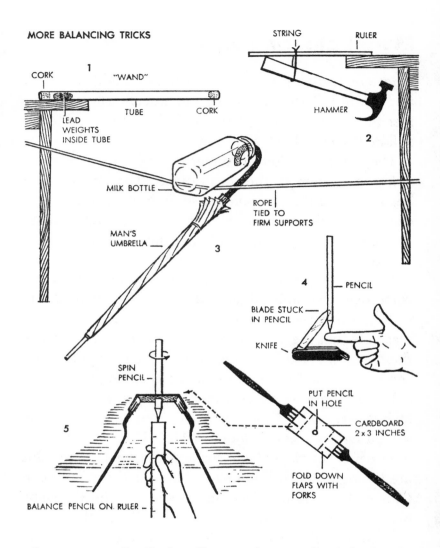

placing an umbrella handle into the mouth of the bottle, as shown.

The center of gravity of this arrangement is quite low, when the bottle is laid across the string. The smooth glass bottle remains securely balanced, much to the amazement of all.

A pencil cannot be balanced on a finger, or anything much smaller, unless the center of gravity is lowered. Try an open penknife whose blade is stuck into the wood, so that the knife handle can be moved under the point of support.

There is another way to balance a pencil. Make a small hole in the center of a 2-by-3-inch piece of heavy cardboard. Stick the pencil through this, to make a tight fit. Attach the prongs of two similar forks on each side of the cardboard. Move the cardboard down to about 2 inches of the point and bend it so that the forks hang low. Move the forks until the pencil balances vertically on your finger. It will also balance on any surface, no matter how narrow. Try it on the head of a small nail.

A real show stopper is to balance the pencil point on the narrow edge of a vertically held ruler. Grasp the eraser part of the pencil and give it a fast spin.

Explain the scientific principle carefully, because everyone will want to make this at home to thrill and amuse the members of the family.

OPTICAL ILLUSIONS

The unbelievable window

Your friends may not believe this astonishing illusion even after you patiently explain it to them. It has appeared on television and has been discussed by psychologists at their professional meetings. This is sure to be the highlight of your science show. And though it takes a little trouble to measure and to cut out of cardboard, it is well worth the time.

It consists of a window with four cut-out "windowpanes," held as shown in the illustration and rotated in one direction by means of an attached dowel. After a few seconds the audience will swear that they see the window moving *back and forth*, from left to right and back again. Yet you insist that you are turning it continuously in one direction in a circle. You call up several assistants to verify this.

Obtain a 12-by-14-inch stiff piece of cardboard which is equally *white* on both sides. Gray cardboard should not be used. Square the corners and then carefully copy the dimensions given in the diagram. Make light guide lines because they will be easier to erase later.

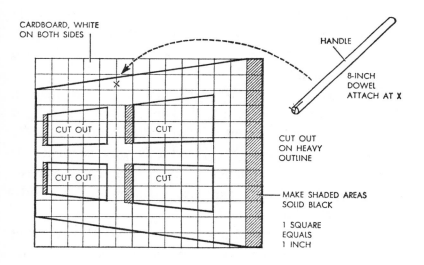

CARDBOARD, WHITE
ON BOTH SIDES

HANDLE

8-INCH
DOWEL
ATTACH AT X

CUT OUT

CUT

CUT OUT

CUT

CUT OUT
ON HEAVY
OUTLINE

MAKE SHADED AREAS
SOLID BLACK

1 SQUARE
EQUALS
1 INCH

Cut out the windowpane sections and blacken the indicated edges. This is to give the cardboard the illusion of thickness when viewed from one direction. Turn the cardboard over and blacken the corresponding edges. Both sides should look alike.

The handle should be about ⅝ inch in diameter, and 8 inches long. Make a slit in the end of the dowel with a saw of the proper thickness, so the paper fits snugly into the slit. If loose, wedge some paper into the slit. Use a nail or glue for fastening the dowel. Make sure that the dowel is parallel to the sides. The handle must be held vertically at all times.

To turn the window, hold the dowel upright, above the window, between the thumb and pointing finger of each hand. Rotate the dowel slowly with these fingers of one hand. As you roll to the ends of your fingers, let the fingers of the other hand take over. With a little practice you can produce a smooth continuous turning. The rate of rotation should be about one complete turn every ten seconds.

You must be at least 10 or 15 feet away from people. The illusion works best in a darkened room. The light should be placed in front so that *both sides are equally illuminated.* A spotlight placed this way is ideal. It helps too for the audience to be in relative darkness. However, this illusion can also be seen under conditions which are not so ideal.

The spectators should not see the prepared window at close range before the show. So if you cannot lay the window flat on a table, far away from prying eyes, keep it hidden in a large manila envelope.

When performing, first ask the audience to please close or cover one eye. Then remove the window from its hidden location, and hold it for an instant so that the audience gets the full view. They will probably think they are seeing a normal window, turned at a slight angle.

Start turning the dowel slowly and smoothly in one direction. After a while ask someone what he sees. He will say that you are turning the window back and forth. You insist that you are turning in only one direction. Invite several spectators to come and see that this is so. Have them tell this to the audience. Get a person to turn the window slowly.

In explaining this illusion, point out that ever since we were babies, we learned that an object seems to get smaller as it goes farther away from us. We call this perspective. We often see a man a block away, who seems to be about a quarter of an inch tall. Yet experience tells us he is a full-sized person.

The window was cut and darkened to appear as a window should in perspective. Our experience tells us that the larger side is the closer side—*even when it may actually be the more distant part of the window.* Every time the window is turned, so that the small side is actually coming toward the audience, the people refuse to believe it. They actually see the large side going away, but their lifetime experience tells them it is coming toward them. The result is that it is easier for people to believe that the operator is moving the window first to one side, and then to the other.

There is an additional part of this demonstration. Place a 15-inch blackened ¼-inch dowel stick through

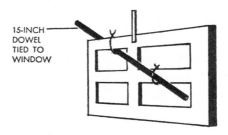

15-INCH DOWEL TIED TO WINDOW

one window, as shown in the illustration. Tie it or wire it into position.

Repeat the experiment as before. Some people will see the stick go through different actions. As the window appears to go back and forth, as it did before, some will see the stick bend or twist this way and that. Some will see the stick appear to go right through the cardboard. However, you will find many who will not see this.

The invisible movie screen

It is always fun to produce "something out of nowhere." Giving a demonstration an occasional magical slant only makes your friends more eager to learn the scientific explanation for which you are preparing them.

Set up a slide or movie projector in a dark room or auditorium. Focus a slide or film on a screen which is facing the audience. Use a picture which has a large and clear object or face. Remove the screen while the projector is on, and mark where the screen was placed when the picture was in focus.

You should be far enough away from a rear wall so that the audience does not see a clear, enlarged image projected on it. It does not matter if they see a very dim, out-of-focus picture. Ask if anybody sees a picture where the screen stood before. Of course, nobody does. Tell the audience that you are now going to produce a screen from out of space.

Do this by waving a ruler or your palm a few feet up and down where the screen should be. Miraculously, a clear picture appears. You make this picture of excellent quality by using a white, lightweight stick, about 1 inch wide, ¼ inch thick, and 30 inches long. The faster you wave, the better the picture will become.

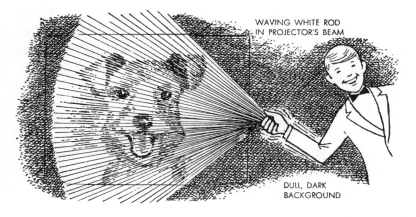

WAVING WHITE ROD
IN PROJECTOR'S BEAM

DULL, DARK
BACKGROUND

You can also obtain a picture by twirling a length of clean white sash cord, which has a heavy knot at the end. However, you will have to swing the rope very fast.

The reason for this illusion is that the eye retains an image of something for about one-sixteenth of a second after it is removed from view. When the waving stick moves quickly to a new position, the eye still sees it in the last position. To emphasize your point, wave the stick slowly at first. Then speed it up and observe the improvement of the picture.

Moving pictures work on the same principle. The projector is designed to show one picture at a time. The pictures are thrown on the screen not slower than sixteen frames per second. The eye still sees the last picture and immediately sees the next one. Since each picture in the film is a little different from one before it, the illusion of motion is created.

Try to slow up a movie machine so that it projects less than sixteen frames per second on a screen. Then you can see these individual pictures. Ask somebody who knows about projectors how to reduce the speed on your machine. Frequently this can be done by a slight pressure on the motor pulley. Other machines may have suitable speed controls.

There is another method of showing that an image persists on the sensitive part of the eye called the retina. It is the bird in the cage illusion. To improve visibility make the heavy white cardboard 8 inches wide and about 12 inches high.

Draw a dark, filled-in figure of a large bird on one side. On the other side make a cage. Use heavy dark lines. You might also wish to make a similar paddle,

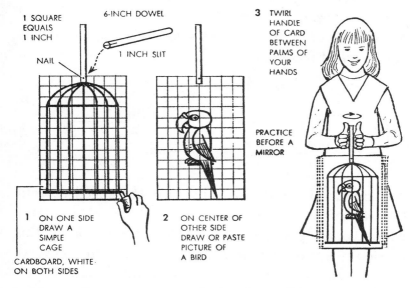

1 SQUARE
EQUALS
1 INCH

6-INCH DOWEL

NAIL

1 INCH SLIT

3 TWIRL
HANDLE
OF CARD
BETWEEN
PALMS OF
YOUR
HANDS

PRACTICE
BEFORE A
MIRROR

1 ON ONE SIDE
DRAW A
SIMPLE
CAGE

CARDBOARD, WHITE
ON BOTH SIDES

2 ON CENTER OF
OTHER SIDE
DRAW OR PASTE
PICTURE OF
A BIRD

having a horse on one side, and a rider on the other side.

Saw a groove in the end of a ½-inch dowel. Slip the cardboard into it, and nail it in place. Roll the dowel between the palms with the cardboard side down. This allows your audience to see both sides in rapid order.

Rubberizing a pencil

Show the audience how you can create an amusing optical illusion by making an ordinary pencil bend as though it were made of rubber. For best results and visibility use a new yellow pencil.

Hold it horizontally between the thumb and index

93

finger. The grip should be very, very loose. Make the pencil flop up and down, as you move your arm up and down for a distance of about 4 inches. *Do not wiggle the pencil with your fingers.*

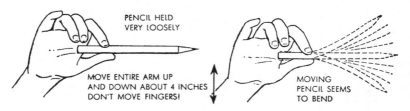

Look closely at the pencil. Vary the speed of your bent arm, until the pencil seems to bend at the place where your fingers hold it. As soon as you achieve this illusion, you can maintain it by continuing to do everything in the same way. With very little practice you will be able to do it perfectly.

Offer to teach the audience how to do this. Get about ten people up on the stage and hand each a pencil. Have them face the audience while you face the participants. Tell them the instructions given above. See who does this first. Give him the pencil as his prize.

This illusion is created because here, too, the eye continues to see an image for a brief instant after the object is no longer there.

Fun with a whisk broom

Call up an assistant and show her a whisk broom. Ask if

she knows what it is called. Give her the answer if she cannot identify it by name. In any event, ask her to spell "whisk." Very few youngsters can do it correctly. However, everybody recognizes what it is used for.

Now place her so that she has her back to you, while the audience is on her right. Ask her to look straight ahead of her. Let her see that the whisk broom is in your right hand. Then pretend to brush her back. Actually she does not see that you are going over her back lightly with your left hand. The brushing sound is made as you *brush yourself!*

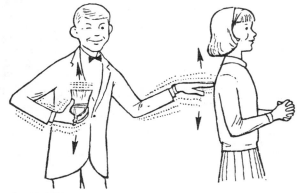

The audience sees this, and enjoys the joke. Stop before she catches on, and ask her what you were doing. She will say that you brushed her. Repeat the stunt, and this time have her turn around while you are in the process of brushing yourself.

When the laughter subsides, talk about the danger of jumping to conclusions, and how our former experiences help us to be fooled. The illusion had to do with the ear, so it can be called an auditory illusion.

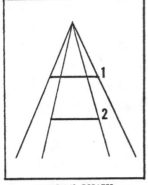

WHICH IS GREATER —
LINE 1 OR LINE 2?

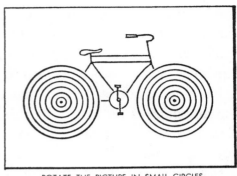

ROTATE THE PICTURE IN SMALL CIRCLES;
THE WHEELS WILL SEEM TO ROTATE TOO.

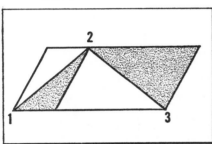

WHICH IS GREATER —
LINE 1-2 OR LINE 2-3?

WHICH IS GREATER —
THE HEIGHT OR BREADTH OF THE HAT?

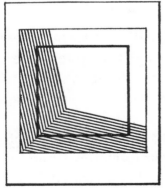

IS THIS A PERFECT SQUARE?

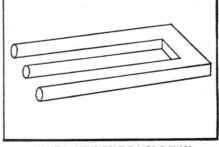

WHAT HAPPENS TO THE MIDDLE TUBE?

King-size optical illusions

There are many fascinating optical illusions which appear in books. These can be drawn on large sheets of white cardboard, so that big audiences can enjoy them all together. For good visibility use dark, heavy lines. Display the cards in a strong light. Have a ruler handy for measuring lines to settle arguments.

Here are some special teasers to start your collection.

SOUND

What made that sound?

Every sound has a different quality, depending upon what is vibrating. From infancy we learn by experience to distinguish these particular vibrations. We can recognize our father's footsteps, even before we see him entering the door. We can distinguish the voice of a friend in the middle of a noisy crowd. We know when a nickel falls to the floor, and when a dime drops.

Audiences love contests and guessing games. Introduce the idea that each sound has its own quality and that you are now going to find out who has the sharpest ears in the audience. First arrange some kind of screen, so nobody can see how your assistant will make the sounds. It is best for you to remain in front, to keep the show moving along.

A screen can be made by cutting away the side of a very large carton. Stand the remaining vertical sides on a table, in front of your props. You may also use a folding screen, or even a bed sheet, held between two sticks lashed to the table legs.

Ask the audience to please remain very quiet while each sound is being made. They are to guess what

causes the sound. Give the answer after each trial. Ask the persons who were correct to raise their hands. After all the sounds are made, find out who got one wrong, two wrong, etc. Make the winner feel important with your lavish praise. Present this person with an inexpensive funny prize. Give the poorest guesser a consolation prize, also of a humorous nature.

Make up your own list of sounds. Here are some to start you off: tearing of paper, cloth, or cardboard; snipping of scissors, sawing of wood, gurgling of water leaving a bottle, turning of an egg beater, sandpapering, sharpening a pencil, releasing air through stretched neck of an inflated balloon, hammering of nail, blowing across bottles, tapping and snapping of fingers, swishing of whisk broom, music of rhythm-band instruments, and the smacking sound of biting into an apple.

If you have access to a tape recorder, you can pre-record many other sounds, including those made out-of-doors. Examples: banging of refrigerator door, hissing of steam radiator, noise of a sanitation truck, flapping of window shades in a draft, idling and racing of an automobile engine, sounds of animals. Include the sound of a barking dog. Ask which animal made the sound and, of course, everybody will say it was a dog.

To make everyone scream with laughter, tell them it is indeed true that the animal sound they just heard was a dog's. But since you could not find a real dog who would cooperate with you during your recording, you asked Mr. Blank (a popular teacher) to make this realistic imitation. Mr. Blank may even be enough of a sport to stand up and take a bow. (Or ask him to take a bow-wow!)

This kind of a program is an ideal place to demonstrate various sound effects used on radio. All you need is a microphone, which is usually available. Experiment to find the best location for it. Below is a list of some artificial sound effects which fool people. To make a sound like bacon and eggs frying on the stove, crumple thin, stiff pieces of plastic in the hands. It also sounds like a crackling blaze in the fireplace. If you use a larger piece of cellophane, and squeeze it harder and faster, it will sound like a forest or brush fire.

A gunshot can be imitated by whacking one piece of flat wood against another. Hinge one board on the other. Hold the two boards hinge side up, and bring them down from overhead like an axe. As you suddenly stop, one board will strike the other with a loud report. It sounds also like the cracking of a whip. Machine-gun fire can be imitated by drumming quickly, but irregularly, with two pencils on the bottom of an oatmeal box.

Hang up a long sheet of metal, and bang it with a stick having a pad of cloth or cotton at the end. It will give off a most realistic rumble of thunder. Rain can be imitated by pouring sand, rice, or small seeds against one side of a ping-pong ball. Have the other side of the ball rest against the microphone. Instead of the ball, try taping a slanted piece of cardboard to the microphone. Put a pan underneath to catch the seeds.

The sound of a trotting horse is made by striking the open ends of two half-coconuts against gravel, in an open box. Attach handles to the tops of the coconuts. Practice imitating trots and gallops.

Make up a clever list of your own. Remember that you must first experiment, and then practice these sound effects, if you want to become good at it.

The big ear—
sound experiments
using a microphone

Almost everyone knows that sound is caused by a rapid back-and-forth motion called "vibration." Many experiments can be performed where the sound which is produced can be heard from a distance, and are therefore suitable for large group presentations. However, there are extremely interesting demonstrations which can be heard only by one person, the experimenter. These are rarely shown on science shows.

Have you ever thought of using the microphone, to make a weak sound so loud that it can be heard all through a large room? You can find microphones used everywhere, for public-address systems and for tape recorders. Use these "mikes" as big ears for your very low-level sound demonstrations.

It is not necessary or advisable to give a complete science course in sound. Sometimes it is enough to give just one involved demonstration. However, the audience should be given a reasonable background to understand the science principle you are talking about. So choose only a few of the following activities for building up your act.

Before you go into the low-level sound demonstrations, you may perhaps wish to let the audience hear, and even see large vibrations. Place any thin strip of wood or metal over the edge of the table. Hold it down firmly on the table top, and flip the loose end with the fingers of your free hand. See and hear the vibrations. Different overhanging lengths produce higher or lower tones.

Waft a large paper through the air faster and faster, until you hear a sound. Bang a drum, and let the audience see how cork, rice, or crumpled paper placed on the parchment or rubber top will bounce. Click a toy cricket, or make one from a *large* open tin can. Simply strike the remaining end of the can with something to produce a bad bend in it. Push the bend down from the inside, so that it does not return to its original condition. Put a small light object into the can, and upset the bend from the outside with your finger. The object will fly up into the air, and a loud sound will be heard.

In all cases point out what is actually vibrating; wood, metal, air, etc. Other loud noises can be made by blow-

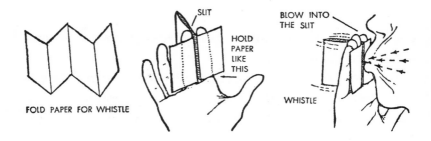

FOLD PAPER FOR WHISTLE

SLIT

HOLD
PAPER
LIKE
THIS

BLOW INTO
THE SLIT

WHISTLE

ing whistles, bursting balloons, twanging large rubber bands or blowing across bottles. Whistles can be made from folded pieces of paper which are held in the hand. Blow into the whistle as shown in the illustration.

Now for some demonstrations producing quiet sounds, for which you will want to use the microphone.

Make a good string telephone by drawing each end of a long string through the center of the bottom of a suitable container. Try stiff paper cups used for hot liquids, and also some cut-down milk cartons. Tie large knots in the ends of the string. When using the telephone always have the string tight. Do not keep your fingers on the string or against the bottom of the container.

Call up two assistants to use the telephone. Have one stand near you. The person at the far end of the phone should be about ten paces away. This may put him outside an open door, and out of sight, but this is good. Instruct the distant helper to say something in a low voice —without using the telephone.

The person near you must be able to say that he does not hear the message. However, he does hear it when the telephone is used. Of course, the loudness of the spoken messages must be the same for each trial.

104

Your job is to keep pointing out these details. Explain all the various substances which are vibrating when using the string telephone; vocal cords, air, bottoms of the containers, string, ear drum, etc. Now ask if the audience would like to hear the message which your assistant claims that he received. Pretend that you just got the bright idea of using the microphone as a big ear.

Hold the open end of the receiver firmly and quietly against the microphone. If the microphone has a small head, put it into the cup. Avoid any motion which will cause a noise in the loud speakers. Again have the distant assistant deliver a long message. Remove the receiver from the microphone several times. The audience must be convinced that the message is louder when the vibrations are being conducted by the string, rather than by air. Do you see how a simple experiment can be worked up into an enjoyable production by the proper use of showmanship?

Another experiment is to start a large fork vibrating by snapping the prongs with a fingernail. Or you may strike a real tuning fork. Hold it near the microphone, but do not allow it to touch. The sound will barely be heard. Snap the fork again and allow the bottom of it to touch the microphone. The sound will be much louder.

Again start the fork vibrating and this time place the bottom of the fork against the cover of a closed cigar box. Hold it close to the microphone. The sound which is produced is louder than when the fork is held in air at the same distance from the microphone. The reason is that the box, and the air inside, are both vibrating at the same rate as the fork. The additional vibrations amplify the sound. Try different forks for best results. Needless to say, all microphone demonstrations *must* be tried in advance. Regulate the volume control of the amplifier. The volume should be as loud as possible, without a disturbing hum or squeal. Also, the best distance at which to hold a sensitive microphone is something you can find out only by experimentation.

How does air conduct sound? Use a length of garden hose, or make a long tube from newspaper by rolling overlapping sheets around a window pole or a broomstick. Talk into one end while the other end is held against the microphone. Show comparisons before and after using the air tube. The sound is louder with the tube because the vibrations are prevented from spreading in all directions as they normally do.

You may use a wooden window pole, or any long stick, to show that wood conducts vibrations better than air. Hold one end of the pole, while an assistant scratches the other end, or taps it lightly with a pencil. You can hardly hear the sound, but when you put your ear to the pole you can hear the scratching sound quite well. Now let the audience hear, by holding your end firmly against the microphone.

Use the microphone to show how a rubber band

produces a higher tone when it is stretched and plucked. To demonstrate that more vibrations per second cause higher tones, run your fingernail over a piece of cloth or a book. Find one with the best weave. The faster you move, the higher will be the tone.

What is the value of large ears to an elephant or a rabbit? Why do we cup our hands around our ears to hear better? Use the microphone to show how sound waves can be channeled to our ears. Do this by placing a large homemade megaphone over the microphone. Compare the loudness of a message without the megaphone and then with it. Incidentally, a distant record player makes a good source of a low sound whose volume remains the same throughout all the tests.

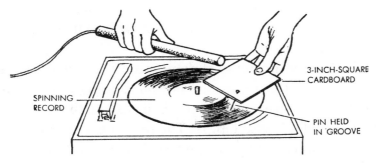

Demonstrate how a phonograph record works. Get an old discarded record, and a record player. Stick a pin into a 3-inch-square piece of cardboard. Hold the cardboard so that the pin is in the grooves as the record turns. Bring a microphone very close to it, or even have it touch the cardboard. The audience will hear the sound very clearly. The wavy grooves in the record cause the pin to vibrate. The card makes the sound louder.

A noisy surprise!

Ask who has had a birthday this month. Give that person a birthday card in an envelope. Say that it is an unusual scientific card, and that you are happy to give it to a deserving person. However, will he please *not* open it until after the show? You do not wish to interrupt the show now.

Continue with your next demonstration, and as sure as God makes little apples, the person is going to open the envelope. It will scare him half to death, and also make everybody else jump. The reason is that the birthday card was booby-trapped with a wound-up noise-maker.

Bend clothes-hanger wire with pliers into the U shape shown in the illustration. It should be 3 inches across and 2 inches deep. Put several small rubber bands across the top. Between the middle of the rubber bands place a heavy piece of cardboard, about 1½ inches by 3 inches. Tape the rubber bands to the middle of the cardboard.

The birthday card is a colorful sheet of cardboard, 6 by 8 inches. Fold the 8-inch side in half. Tape the bottom of the noise-maker about one inch from the top of the right inside section.

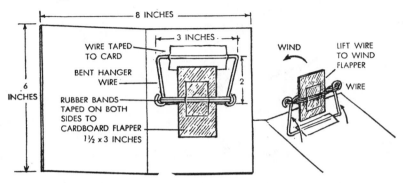

Wind up the flapper very tightly, and close the folded card. Put it into a large envelope, with the open side of the card facing out. When the unsuspecting person pulls it out and opens it, the flapper strikes the card repeatedly as it unwinds.

Write something appropriate on the card and color it. If you can find a suitable commercial birthday card, so much the better.

GRAVITY

The clinging-glass deception

Your friends will know that you are spoofing them, and they will enjoy this hoax immensely. But if you do it properly, they will have a hard time arriving at the correct solution, until you lose patience and give away the secret.

Tell everybody that once on a high mountain in Tibet you saw a Yogi standing on his head. He had two inverted drinking glasses resting on a book. Then when he stood up, he naturally turned the book over too. He found that the glasses were now suspended from the bot-

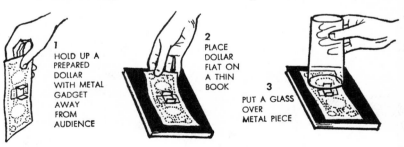

1 HOLD UP A PREPARED DOLLAR WITH METAL GADGET AWAY FROM AUDIENCE

2 PLACE DOLLAR FLAT ON A THIN BOOK

3 PUT A GLASS OVER METAL PIECE

tom of the book! The reason given by the man was that by silent meditation and prayer he could cancel gravity. He taught you how to do it. You would like to show this to everybody.

Take a dollar bill from your wallet or pocket. Hold up the tip of it, so that the rest of the bill hangs down. Place it flat on a small, hard-covered book. Blow into a glass, then rub it on your clothes. Place it upon the dollar, with the open side of the glass down. Now put your thumb against the glass, while the other fingers are under the book. Turn the book upside down, and the glass does not fall.

Say that you spent an extra twenty years learning how to do it with two glasses. Again, go through some fancy hocus-pocus with the glasses, which your imagination can surely dream up. Set the two glasses on the dollar and put your educated thumb between the glasses. The rest of your fingers are again under the book. Invert the setup. As the two glasses remain mysteriously suspended say, "The most difficult thing is to turn everything over and back to the original position."

4 PUT YOUR THUMB AGAINST GLASS

TURN UPSIDE DOWN

5

6 PUT A GLASS OVER EACH METAL PIECE; PRESS THUMB BETWEEN GLASSES

TURN UPSIDE DOWN 7

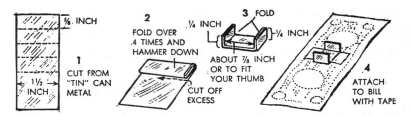

	2	3 FOLD
⅜ INCH	FOLD OVER	
1	.4 TIMES AND	ABOUT ⅞ INCH
CUT FROM	HAMMER DOWN	OR TO FIT
"TIN" CAN		YOUR THUMB
METAL	CUT OFF	
1½ INCH	EXCESS	.4 ATTACH TO BILL WITH TAPE

¼ INCH   ¼ INCH

Make a big to-do about turning the book. Actually it is easy. When you finally do this, remove the glasses. Again pick up the dollar bill by the edge and shake it. Replace it in your wallet or pocket. Let your friends give their solutions. Let them see the glasses, book, and even the dollar!

The secret is a piece of stiff metal, bent as shown in the illustration. Tape it to the back of the dollar, or any opaque paper. When you later pass out the dollar for examination, give them a duplicate bill minus the gimmick!

When the open glass is placed on the metal, it should be inside against the bent-up side of the gimmick. When you press your thumb against the glass, friction will hold it. The second glass should be in a similar position on the opposite side. Practice over a bed. After a few trials you will be an expert.

Incidentally, watch your angles. Either work on a slightly elevated platform or else tilt the book slightly toward you. In this way the audience will not catch a glimpse of the gimmick. Make up your own funny lines to go with the act. It is hilarious to listen to the zany, unscientific guesses of your friends.

The thin metal should be stiff and about a ½ inch

wide. Bend the ¼ inch ends with pliers or in a vise. The distance between the bent ends should be about ⅞ inch. It should be strong enough to resist bending by hand. Look around for the correct strip. If you do not have the proper tools or materials ask some adult to make several gimmicks for you. He can do it in a few minutes.

You can easily make the gimmick yourself from the thin metal of an ordinary tin can. You can cut this with an old pair of scissors. Because it is thin, you will have to bend it over itself four times to give it the proper strength.

Cut a squared-off piece, exactly 1½ inches wide by about 4 inches long. Bend over a half-inch section by hand, line it up square and hammer the bend flat. See illustration. After the fourth bend, cut off the excess. File the ends round. Now use this for making your gimmick.

Gravity-defying trick

Here is a puzzler. It is really a trick, but it is interesting to find out how firmly your audience believes in the law of gravity. Watch them exercise their scientific vocabulary and common sense, as they attempt to explain this antigravity phenomenon.

You show them a bottle, or a narrow-mouthed vase, which is dark or completely opaque. Turn it with the opening down, and give it a shake. Put in the end of a 2

113

foot length of stiff sash rope. Let go of the rope or raise the bottle. Naturally, the rope falls out.

Pretend that you did not shake it enough. Hold the bottle with its mouth down again, and this time shake it strongly. Put in the end of the rope and lift the bottle. Lo and behold, the rope remains suspended in the bottle! Take hold of the rope and let go of the bottle. The audience is surprised to see the rope hold up the bottle and swing it like a pendulum. Finish the trick by re-

moving the rope. You may even hand out the materials for inspection.

The secret is a small cork or rubber ball, which you held in your hand at the start. It was easily inserted when the bottle was placed upside down on your palm for the second shaking. A short unnoticeable tug on the rope wedged the cork or rubber ball against the rope and the bottle neck. Later, you can remove the ball by pulling on the rope with one hand. Your other hand over the bottle neck gets the ball as it is pulled out. Or you may hold the bottle upright and push the rope slightly into the bottle. The freed ball drops into the bottle, and is removed when you turn the bottle upside down over your palm.

The size of the ball depends upon your bottle opening. For example, a ⅝-inch opening and a ¼-inch rope would need a ball about ½ inch in diameter. You must experiment to find the right size for other bottles.

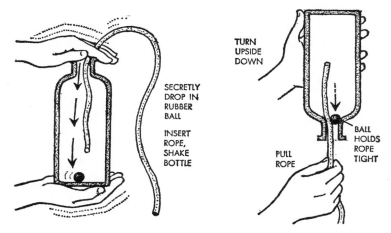

The ball, which need not be perfectly round, is made as follows. First cut a cork, or rubber stopper, into a cube. That is, each side is the same size. This should be the same width as the ball you wish to make. Use scissors to cut a small, but equal bevel (slant) at each of the twelve edges. Now cut a small piece from each of the original eight corners of the cube. Finally, carefully snip away observable unround sections. If you wish, you may file or sandpaper. But it really is not necessary. It may even be better because of the increased friction.

115

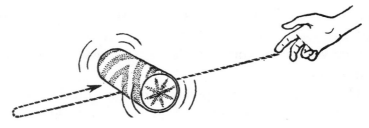

Please come back!

An extremely delightful puzzle is a cylindrical container which you roll away from you on the floor. But when you politely say, "Please come back," the toy dutifully returns to your hand like a playful puppy. You can also make it do other tricks.

You may construct this from all kinds of cylindrical containers, such as covered coffee cans, oatmeal boxes, and various sizes of paper cylinders for taking home food from delicatessen stores, Chinese restaurants, or coffee shops. You might even try the drum-sized containers used for ice cream or for chemicals at your druggist. Paint these with various colors and designs, such as spirals or rings which have an intriguing appearance when they roll.

The illustration shows a quart-size paper container *with parallel sides*. Many containers are wider at the top. These will return to you in a curve. There are two 1-ounce lead fishing weights tied to the middle of several rubber bands. The ends have been drawn through the exact center of the container's cover and bottom. Use a doubled-over length of wire or a looped string to help you do this.

The rubber bands are prevented from being drawn into the box by a nail or match stick placed on the outside, through the loops. If the nail turns, tape it into position. Adjust the weights and rubber bands so that the weights never touch the side of the container.

Here is how the roll-back toy works. The freely hanging weight is being pulled down by gravity. As you roll the cylinder away from you on the floor, the rubber bands get wound up because of the forward motion of the container. The weight prevents any unraveling. Energy is stored up by the winding rubber bands, until the box slows down. The energy of the wound-up "spring" makes the box return, as the weight continues to pull down.

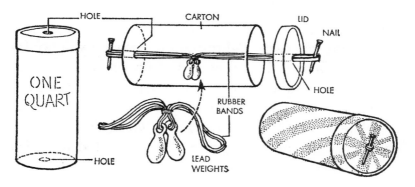

Using several thin rubber bands is often better than using one—which may break and put you out of business. Use any weights, such as heavy nuts or bolts, but fishing weights are most practical. They have holes and are heavy, and can be hammered into shorter shapes if they scrape the bottom. They are bought very cheaply

117

at hardware or sports shops. Use the best weight for the size of your container.

Before giving the audience your explanation, pretend that the toy comes back because you say the magic word "Please." Then have it return without saying, "Please." Ask if anybody thinks that there is a little man inside. Finally tell the reason in detail. Pull out the cover a short distance, so the rubber bands are visible. If possible, make a model from a clear plastic cylinder.

An amusing stunt with this toy is to say that you will now demonstrate how the container behaves when it gets dizzy. Hold one end of the container while it is in a vertical position, and twirl it in a small circle. You will feel the weights swinging around as the bands are wound up. Finally set the container *vertically* on the table or any *smooth* surface.

The box will twist and turn, but it usually will not fall until *just before* the rubber band unwinds completely. Then it will suddenly fall over on its side. After a few advance trials, you will be able to time your remarks, and know exactly when the fall is going to occur. At that moment you may pretend to shoot it dead. The coincidence is startling.

This twisting effect is improved by not tying the weights in the middle of the rubber bands. With the weights off center, try this stunt with first one end up and then the other. You will get very different results.

Instead of putting down the hand-wound container in a vertical position, lay it down on its side on the floor. It will bang and jerk and seem to move in a most unwilling manner. Make up a suitable patter for this effect. Call it a temper tantrum, or "This is how I feel about going to school," etc.

If you decide to use a metal can for this toy, protect the rubber bands from being cut where they leave the cover. Wrap a small strip of adhesive plaster over the rubber. Or you may use an enlarged hole and center the rubber in it. Try using some of your mother's flat or round elastic tape. It may be longer-lasting than rubber.

ENTERTAINING
SMALL GROUPS

Most demonstrations you have read about thus far have been designed for use with larger audiences. Of course, you may use these for small intimate groups too. However, the following stunts are best done for individual friends or at parties. They are smaller, or have decreased visibility for other reasons.

The leaping coin

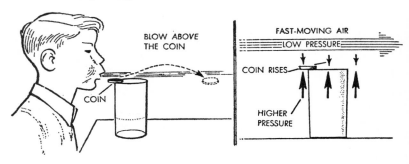

Set a drinking glass near the edge of a table. Carefully place a large coin flat on the side of the rim nearest you. Bend down and say you are going to blow the coin over the glass. Then you proceed to do this with the utmost ease. You challenge anybody to repeat this. Many people will try, but unless they know the secret, they are doomed to failure.

Naturally, your smug friends will first try to get under the coin, and blow it up and over the glass. This is the worst thing they can do. The coin will only fall repeatedly into the glass, to the utter frustration of the experimenters. Have many glasses and coins, so that the entire group can be engaged in this hilarious activity. Every once in a while, show everybody how easily you do it each time you try.

Oddly enough, the secret is to blow a short distance *over* the coin, with a fast horizontal gust. The mouth should be close to the coin. After a little practice, you will be able to make a half dollar leap over a bathtub.

Your success is due to the Bernoulli effect, whereby a rapidly moving stream of air produces a low-pressure space around it. Your fast breath over the top of the coin produces an air pressure lower than that on the bottom of the coin. The higher air pressure underneath the coin now pushes the coin up. The strength of your breath also pushes the coin across the glass.

Hindoo rope trick

Folklore reports that in India street magicians do a marvelous rope trick. First a rope is thrown to the ground. Then the rope stiffens and rises vertically far into the air. The magician's assistant then climbs up this rope and disappears.

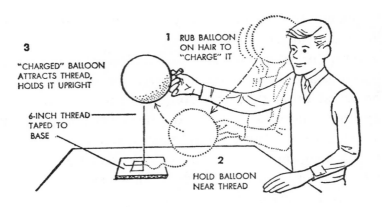

3

"CHARGED" BALLOON
ATTRACTS THREAD,
HOLDS IT UPRIGHT

1 RUB BALLOON
ON HAIR TO
"CHARGE" IT

6-INCH THREAD
TAPED TO
BASE

2

HOLD BALLOON
NEAR THREAD

The magician calls him down, but there is no response. Finally, he angrily climbs up the rope with a sword in his hand. He too disappears, and angry words are heard above. Cut-up pieces of legs, arms, and other parts of the boy's body come raining down.

The magician climbs down, alone of course, and puts the pieces of the boy into a sack. After some magic words, the sack is opened, and out steps the boy, smiling and in one piece. No scientist has ever seen this done. Psychologists believe the reports of the spectators are the result of group hypnotism.

Your audience will enjoy such stories as introductions to your demonstrations. Just for fun, tell them you will do your own version of the "Hindoo rope trick." It is really an effect of static electricity.

In the center of a 3-inch square of cardboard, tape or tie the end of a lightweight, thin length of colored string. Use about 6 inches at first. Now rub an inflated balloon on your hair. Or you may use a small plastic cheese container, or anything else to charge up.

Hold it near and above the rope so that it tries to stand straight up. You may have to cut off some of the string, until you have the longest length capable of being attracted upward and remaining that way. The string must *not* touch your charged object. You can make the string sway mysteriously. This works best on dry, cool days. The best string consists of one or two strands pulled out of a light package string.

"Smoke" from mouth

This is a real puzzler—even to your friends who know science. Tell them that you can get smoke from your mouth any time you want to. Of course, this is without smoking a cigarette or anything so obvious. Even offer to rinse your mouth, or drink some water before the display.

Anybody can do this—but it takes a few minutes of practice. Hold your lips tightly closed, and build up a strong pressure of air inside your mouth by attempting to exhale. Do not allow air to escape from the nostrils. Really force the breath from your lungs, and let your cheeks and lips blow up.

In a few seconds you will feel that the breath in your mouth has been strongly compressed. Open your lips slowly and let the compressed air escape slowly, either by itself or pushed forward by the tongue. You will see a slight wisp of "smoke." *Under no conditions must you allow the breath to escape suddenly or explosively.*

The tiny amount of "smoke" is best seen in good artificial light or sunlight.

As you have probably guessed, the smoke is really condensed water vapor. When you build up a pressure, you are compressing warm, moisture-laden air from your lungs. A sudden release of pressure cools the air enough to condense the water vapor and form a tiny cloud.

You can get the same effect in a glass gallon jug. Blow hard into it, with your lips tightly pressed against the opening. Then suddenly remove your lips, and some of the water vapor condenses in the jug.

Bent spoon illusion

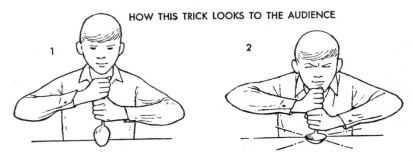

HOW THIS TRICK LOOKS TO THE AUDIENCE

1   2

You can create a remarkable illusion that you are bending a spoon. Do it across the table facing your observer. Hold the spoon vertically against the table, with the handle side up. The hollow part of the spoon should be toward your audience. Enclose your left fist around the spoon, above the bowl part. Place your right fist around the upper part of the handle, above the left fist. The knuckles of both hands must be in a vertical line. Now

124

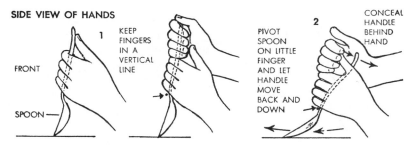

SIDE VIEW OF HANDS

FRONT

SPOON

1 KEEP FINGERS IN A VERTICAL LINE

PIVOT SPOON ON LITTLE FINGER AND LET HANDLE MOVE BACK AND DOWN

2

CONCEAL HANDLE BEHIND HAND

pretend you are going to bend the spoon against the table. However, you must release the spoon from all your fingers but the bottom small one. Use this finger as a hinge, while you swing the top of the spoon toward you. This movement is hidden by both fists.

This illusion must be viewed from the front. It looks best when the front of both fists makes a vertical wall *at all times during the "bending."*

Stopping pulse at will

Tell the audience that there are certain mystics in India who allow themselves to be placed alive in coffins, and buried underground for some length of time. They claim that they do this by suspending animation; that is, they practically stop living. This means very little breathing and hardly any heartbeat, etc.

Say that you too can stop your pulse at will by sheer concentration. Get an assistant who knows how to take one's pulse at the wrist. Give him a baton or pencil, and tell him to beat time with your pulse. Explain to everyone that the pulse is a surge of blood through your arter-

125

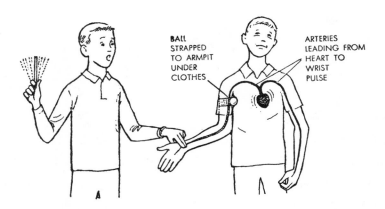

BALL STRAPPED TO ARMPIT UNDER CLOTHES

ARTERIES LEADING FROM HEART TO WRIST PULSE

ies every time your heart beats. As the assistant's pencil moves up and down, you say you will now stop your pulse. You do just that, much to everybody's amazement.

The trick is done by strapping an ordinary rubber ball to the inside part of your upper arm, just below the armpit. There is an artery there which carries blood for the wrist pulse. The ball is hidden by your clothing, and you can squeeze it secretly to harmlessly stop your pulse for a few seconds. Use adhesive plaster for holding the ball in place. Try this trick on both arms.

Incidentally, the Indian trick does not involve stopping the heart. The buried man simply keeps extremely calm, and breathes very, very slowly. In this way he uses very little oxygen. If the heart stops beating for a very brief interval, a person will die. That is because delicate vital regions in the brain will not receive fresh blood and oxygen which the heart pumps around. Then these brain cells quickly lose their ability to maintain body functions which control life.

A handy wand

You can quickly make a small, bewitching, fairy wand to add glamour to your tricks. Flatten a long, colorful drinking straw, and make eleven even, but alternate folds in it. These accordian pleats should be about ½-inch long.

Arrange the sections to form a five-pointed star. Crimp the two ends, and wedge them into the top of another straw. You can make other figures too with pipe-cleaner wire or folded paper. Vary the sizes.

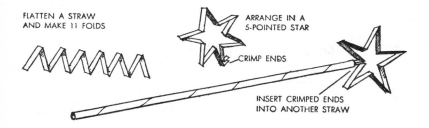

FLATTEN A STRAW
AND MAKE 11 FOLDS

ARRANGE IN A
5-POINTED STAR

CRIMP ENDS

INSERT CRIMPED ENDS
INTO ANOTHER STRAW

Static-electricity detector

Cut a sheet of light cardboard 2 by 8 inches. Fold it in half the long way. Balance the lower part on a pencil point. Make a dimple at the pivot. Better still, use a small dress snap, from which the vertically-held pencil will not slip out.

Hold the pencil up by sticking it in a hole in wood, clay, eraser, etc. Rub a balloon, plastic or hard-rubber comb, on hair, cloth, or other substances. When held

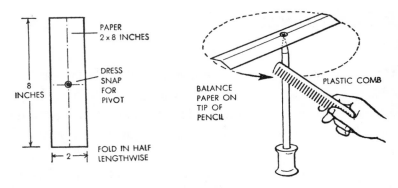

PAPER
2 x 8 INCHES

DRESS
SNAP
FOR
PIVOT

8
INCHES

FOLD IN HALF
LENGTHWISE

2

BALANCE
PAPER ON
TIP OF
PENCIL

PLASTIC COMB

near one end of your detector, the paper will turn toward or away from you.

The paper balances so well because, as you learned before, most of the weight is below the point of support.

The suspended paper clip

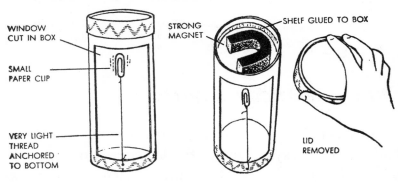

WINDOW
CUT IN BOX

SMALL
PAPER CLIP

VERY LIGHT
THREAD
ANCHORED
TO BOTTOM

STRONG
MAGNET

SHELF GLUED TO BOX

LID
REMOVED

In this display a paper clip is attached to a thread and apparently defies gravity. The clip is up in mid-air, while the other end of the thread is anchored to the bottom of an oatmeal box. A window is cut in front of the box.

The illustration shows you the secret. A very strong alnico horseshoe magnet is hidden on a shelf which is glued underneath the top cover, and above the window of the box.

The steel paper clip should be small and lightweight. The thread must be very thin and also light in weight. There is a limit, of course, to the height of the thread, since it has weight. Experiment to find the best position for the magnet in the secret compartment. Tape it into the final position. The farther away the clip is from any part of the box, the more spectacular this display becomes.

Hole in the hand

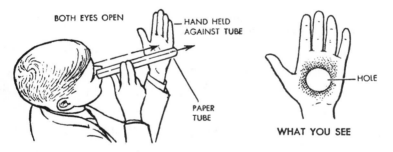

Give each person a sheet of paper and ask him to curl it into a 1-inch tube. Have him hold the tube in his right hand and look through it with his right eye. The left eye is also open. At the same time, his left palm is held vertically alongside the end of the tube.

He will see a large, clear hole right through his left palm. The reason is that each of our eyes always sees a separate image. However, beyond a certain distance, our brain combines them into one picture. Because the left hand and the hole are closer than the needed focus, the person now sees separate images of the hand and the hole.

Baffling T puzzle

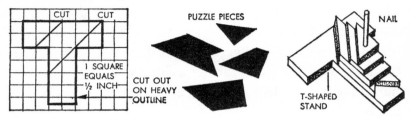

Make up many of these puzzles from cardboard to hand out to your friends. Mix up the four pieces and ask the contestants to make a perfect letter T. Give them a very fast glimpse of one you make and quickly disarrange. This puzzle is most frustrating to everyone. Many people will find it impossible to do.

Make some of thin wood. The size does not matter, as long as the proportions are like those in the illustration. If you wish, you may make a small stand to hold the pieces. Holes in each piece slip over a vertical nail. The base is the exact size and shape of the finished T.

Name game

Make up your own rules for this game. Play it by choosing teams, or having everybody doing it on his own, to see who completes it first.

Rule a sheet, or do it on a blackboard as shown below. If you wish, you may make other categories.

	ANIMALS	FLOWERS	FRUITS	VEGETABLES
S				
P				
I				
N				

The word "spin" on the left, is a word picked out of a hat containing many others. The game is played by placing this selected word vertically on the left, so that one letter is next to a line. Players take turns filling in each space with any correct word which starts with the letter next to the line.

For example, an animal starting with S is snake. A flower could be a snapdragon, and a fruit is strawberry. The word "spinach" could be inserted in the vegetable column.

Funny displays

Have an empty jar on display. Label it DEHYDRATED WATER. It is unbelievable how long some people will contemplate this before they realize the joke.

Another display is a jar of clear water. The sign should say INVISIBLE GLASS FISH FROM SUMATRA. You will be astonished at the number of people who will say they are seeing fish.

Or have a sign on a metal can or an opaque jar which reads WOULD YOU LIKE TO SEE SOMETHING NOBODY EVER SAW BEFORE? The jar contains some kind of inexpensive, unshelled nut. The spectator cracks the nut, and now becomes the first person to see the kernel inside.

Have a display of unusual scientific conversation pieces. For example, for a few cents you can buy eyeglasses for a chicken. They are sold at Sears-Roebuck, Montgomery Ward, or at some chicken-feed supply stores.

These are hooked through the high nostrils of a chicken. The purpose is to obstruct the vision and to prevent other chickens from harming other egg-laying chickens, on whose tail feathers some blood is sometimes seen. Chickens, as well as some tropical fish, often molest and even kill sick companions.

A popular display is a closed candy box containing a 4-inch cylindrical pole. The spectator is supposed to guess what is in the box, turning it in all directions, and listening to the sounds made inside. Disclose the answer in some interesting manner. Try enclosing other objects in the candy box.

PRACTICAL JOKES

There are many harmless practical jokes you can play on your friends. At the right time, and in the right place, these scientific tricks can have much entertainment value.

The disappearing paper

Have your friend stand facing you while you roll up a paper napkin or a handkerchief. Pretend to hide it in one of your closed hands. Ask him to guess in which fist you have it. After a few trials, throw it over his shoulder and immediately close your hand again.

Again ask him in which hand you have the napkin. He will guess one hand. Show him that it is empty. Naturally, he thinks that the paper is now hidden in the other hand. Make a big fuss about making it vanish. Finally open your empty hand and enjoy his surprise.

Now get next to him and stand in the same direction he is standing. Put your closed right hand up, and away from you. Ask him to look closely at your closed hand. Keep up a constant flow of patter. Meanwhile, your left hand is cupped behind you in a natural manner, ready to receive the paper your secret assistant has picked up and is going to hand you. Put your right and left hands together and make the paper reappear. Everybody is on to the secret—except the person being fooled.

This trick always works if the person you are doing it to has never seen it done. When you throw the paper over his shoulder, his eyes automatically close. This is a defense mechanism on the part of the eyes.

A harmless smelling trick

Show your friend a small plastic bottle or vial containing some water. Remove the cover and smell the water. Act puzzled and replace the stopper. Ask if he has a good "smeller" and can identify peculiar odors. As he removes the cover, a very fine stream of water comes out of the container and harmlessly drips over his shoes or clothing.

TIGHT LID
WATER
HOLE
SNIFF WATER; KEEP HOLE COVERED
LID

REPLACE LID TIGHTLY HAND CONTAINER TO A FRIEND

WATER SPRAYS FROM HOLE AS LID IS REMOVED

The secret is that there is a tiny hole at the bottom of the container's side. When the top is airtight, the water is held inside. But when the cover is removed, the air pressure and weight of the water make the fine stream escape.

When filling the small container, and also when smelling it, keep your finger over the hole until you close the top tightly. Hand it to your friend with the hole side toward him. Ask him to keep his eyes closed, since you "think this sharpens one's sense of smell."

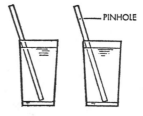

PINHOLE

An unfair contest

Have a contest to see who can sip up water fastest through a straw. Give each person the same amount of drinking water in a clean container. Build up the winner with much praise, so that he will feel very proud of himself.

135

Have another sipping race using new straws. See that the former winner chooses a straw in which you have secretly made a pin-hole about 2 inches from the top. Make sure the straw is used in that position. Needless to say, the former winner will lose miserably. Unless you tell him why, he may never know, since the hole is not easily detected.

A drinking straw works because a person shapes his cheeks so that the air pressure in the straw is lessened. The normal air pressure on the water in the glass is now greater than the air pressure inside the straw. The water in the straw is therefore driven toward the lower pressure above it in the straw, and into the mouth.

The small hole does not allow your frustrated friend to remove air from the straw. Fresh air keeps coming in.

Testing strength with magnets

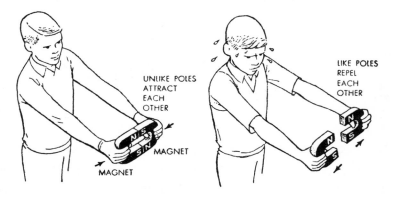

Obtain two strong horseshoe magnets of the same size. Hold one magnet in each hand. Show everybody how you can put the two magnets together at arm's length, while your elbows are locked.

Ask for a volunteer to duplicate your feat. Unless he knows the trick he cannot do it, because you reversed one magnet as you handed both to him. When you did it, you had opposite poles touch. These of course, attracted each other. The volunteer tries to do it by putting similar poles together.

This is very difficult to do with strong magnets. Also, the arms are in a very weak position when working toward each other at arm's length.

Inverted glass of water

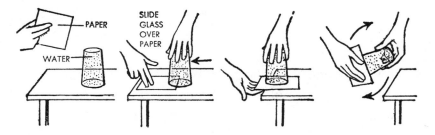

Prepare this trick secretly before your friends come. Fill a glass with water almost to the top, and put a thin cardboard over it. Invert it and set it on a table having a plastic top, such as formica. Hold the glass down while you pull out the cardboard and hide it. Inexperienced people will look upon this upturned glass of water with alarm. They will not know how to remove the glass without using a pan or creating a mess.

The easy way to remove the inverted glass of water is to lay a thin piece of cardboard on the table near it. Slide the glass over it and draw it partly over the edge of the table. Place one hand under the cardboard, and the other hand on top of the glass. Now turn over the glass.

Do not use a wooden table, because of possibility of damage to the surface.

Blowing watery bubbles

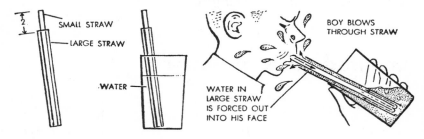

Show someone what large bubbles you can create in a glass of water by blowing through a straw. Ask your friend to try doing this. Give him a new straw. But when he blows, he gets his face splashed with water.

The horrible truth is that you gave this poor fellow a gimmicked straw. Make one up by placing a smaller straw inside a larger one of the same color. The outside, larger straw should be about 2 inches below the top of the inside straw.

When your friend blows into this straw, you should hold it naturally and lightly press it down to the bottom of the glass. When he blows hard into the small straw,

138

he is also driving some air into the bottom of the larger
straw. This increases the pressure in the larger tube.
Since there is water in this part of the tube, it is driven
up to the surprised person's face.

Curiosity killed the cat

Have a toy telescope or a pair of opera glasses on a table.
A sign states PLEASE DO NOT USE THIS INSTRUMENT. Of
course, people *will* pick it up and put it to their eyes—
but they will be embarrassingly sorry! Before you know
it several people will be walking around with harmless
black rings around their eyes. They will wonder where
they got the "shiners."

But you know, don't you? You used some of your big
sister's mascara to smear around the eyepiece. Or you
might use carbon, made by holding a cold dish or spoon
over a candle flame.

This is an excellent lesson in psychology. People also
insist upon testing painted surfaces, even though a sign
clearly states WET PAINT.

How observant are you ?

Make a very strong salt solution. Place your finger into it, and then lick your finger. Show that you enjoyed it. Ask someone else to taste the liquid. They will find it unappetizing.

The secret is that you dipped your middle finger into the salt water. But when you tasted it, you switched fingers, and licked your index finger.

Try different solutions. It is interesting how unobservant people are. Rub your finger on your shoe, and stick the switched one into your mouth. Lick your finger thoroughly, exclaiming that the shoe tastes very sweet.

The suspended pencil

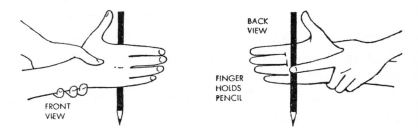

Have the back of your right hand facing the audience while your left hand holds your right wrist. Hold a pencil vertically in the middle of your right palm by means of the left index finger, as shown in the illustration.

The pencil will seem to the audience to be mysteriously suspended by some unseen force. However, somebody will probaby know this old trick, and say that your hidden finger is holding up the pencil. You turn around and let everybody see that your finger is really holding the pencil.

Turn back to the original position, and this time remove your entire left hand from your right wrist. The audience will gasp when they see the pencil still suspended as before.

Give a lecture on how unscientific it is to jump to conclusions. Get the people to agree that they were wrong before, especially the person who previously said that your finger was holding the pencil.

Finally, give away the secret. Did you guess it? A 1-inch strip of clear plastic tape is placed partly on the pencil, and partly on your palm!

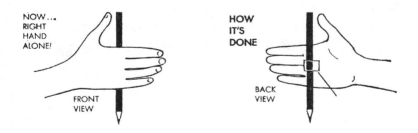

The water-pail hoax

Get a toy pail. Pour in some water, and swing the pail overhead and around in a large vertical circle. Ask why

POUR A GLASS OF WATER INTO A PAIL

WHIRL FAST, THEN SLOWLY

HOLD STILL OVERHEAD

NO WATER!

THE SECRET

SPONGE GLUED TO BOTTOM OF PAIL

the water does not spill out. You will no doubt get the proper answers.

Repeat the demonstration many times. Say that each time you will swing the pail more slowly. Finally, swing the pail overhead so slowly that any water inside would simply have to pour down on you. In fact, at one point stop the upturned pail overhead.

No water pours out! No wonder—you had cemented a large absorbent sponge on the bottom of the pail!

OTHER TYPES
OF SCIENCE SHOWS

There are many kinds of shows which have scientific themes. In this chapter you may get an idea which you can discuss and work up with your friends. You can make up a program which is highly interesting and informative to all. You may even inspire someone to want to learn more about the fascinating field of science.

But regardless of which program is selected for presentation, remember to observe the main ideas you learned about showmanship. In this way you will be sure that you are getting the best results from your efforts.

Science hobby show

This is a very popular show and is always sure of success. It is done by the combined efforts of many people, so the burden does not fall on you. The participants are very enthusiastic about their pastimes. They love to talk about them, and always have something unusual to show. The glow of their excitement makes eager listen-

143

ers of all their friends in the audience. This, of course, has tremendous entertainment value.

Round up half a dozen science hobbyists. These may include chemistry-set enthusiasts; pigeon breeders; hamster, rabbit, and mouse raisers; and snake, frog, or lizard collectors. Good talks and demonstrations can be given by bird watchers, geologists ("rock hounds"), ham radio operators, model-airplane builders, and scores of other people who know how to enjoy their leisure time to the utmost.

One of the best techniques for presenting this assortment of talent and earnestness, is for you to become the Master of Ceremonies, popularly called the M.C. You must introduce each one in a refreshing, enticing manner. Then you proceed to ask very informal questions: How did you get interested in your hobby? Is it expensive? Where do you work in your home? Is your mother annoyed because of the mess? What do you like best about your hobby? What did you bring to show us? Tell your performers to bring large items and to talk in a loud, clear, unhurried voice. Try to invite spectacular acts. For example, the boy who raises homing pigeons may send a message home to his mother, telling what he wants for lunch. He ties the message to the pigeon's leg and releases it outside a window.

The ham operator may bring a walkie-talkie, to converse with a friend far away. The snake collector may show a harmless snake which can be touched by spectators to convince them that it is not slimy. The bird watcher can bring a model platform bird feeder or imitate bird calls. The "rock hound" may show some fluorescent rocks under an ultraviolet light.

Can you see the enormous possibilities of this kind of show? Many people develop an interest in a hobby, once they see it presented this way. But above all, a clever M.C. can do himself proud.

Best of science fair

Almost every school has a science fair every year. For presentation, select the better ones—especially the larger exhibits. Use the same treatment you did for the hobby show.

As M.C., you must get the participant to point out the important parts. Ask questions about the scientific principles. Talk in a friendly, conversational manner. Pretend that you do not know as much science as you really do. In this way you force the exhibitor to explain things more simply. Then everybody in the audience will understand.

Pet shows

Most of us have some kind of pet at home. We love it, and have probably taught it to do some kind of simple trick. We have read much about the care, feeding, and upbringing of the lovable creature. We welcome the chance to bring it before a group and "show off."

Perhaps you think that this type of show needs more room, and should be done out-of-doors, when the weather gets warm. Then you can have an animal parade, with all kinds of colorful costumes, buggies, and carts. Later, you can seat everybody in a semicircle, and arrange some kind of stage area for the show.

Ask the participants interesting questions. Is a fish or bird an animal? How does a pet snake move? Why is your highpitched whistle only heard by your dog? Are dogs descendants of wolves? Why do turtles often get soft shells? Can your dog do a trick? What do you call your pet? What do you feed it?

If the dog is particularly frisky, have an adult bring it to the show. Get rid of the slightest trace of trouble immediately.

Dramatizations

It is fun to make up a science play, to be acted out by you and your friends. Choose a theme such as an incident in the life of a famous scientist. Dramatize the discovery or invention of something important in science. Write a play about being kind to animals, or conserving wild life, or about Arbor Day.

Some plays can be very imaginative. Pretend that suddenly there is no more electricity in your community. Or suppose you were living on Mars. Act out the happenings in your city if the drinking water became dangerously polluted with poison. Somebody once wrote a play about the day all the birds left his town. Another dreamed up a splendid play about all the things that happened to the world because it was not rotating for some mysterious reason.

"What is it?" show

The show starts with a long table covered by a large bedsheet. You explain that under the cover you have large objects you want each person to identify with the correct name.

If the group is small, give each individual a pencil and some paper. Ask the audience to number from one to twenty-five. As you show each item, they write the name next to the correct number. Tell them it will spoil the fun to speak or to copy from one another.

After you get through showing all the objects, you pick each one up again. This time you name it correctly. Since you have a captive audience, you can tell many scientific facts, such as the origin and use of each object. If a scientific principle is involved, tell about that too. This is an ideal way of getting interest.

If the audience is large, you should not attempt to have them take tests and mark their papers. Instead, you can ask for volunteers to answer when you hold up each object. You might have a team of boys play against a team of girls. Have them seated on the stage. Make up your own simple rules for the contest.

You can easily see that for this show to be successful, large, interesting objects must be used. Do not make the contest too difficult. The item should be something the audience has heard about, or knows a little about what it is used for, but they may not know the name. Look up each item in an encyclopedia, or get very interesting information about it some other way. Look around for unusual, but not unheard-of articles.

Here are some suitable objects: binoculars, a snake plant, a pulley, stick of bamboo, cricket (metal-snapping noise-maker), a large stuffed bird, a funnel, trowel, blue print, aneroid barometer, large screw eye, glass prism, vacuum bottle, wooden salad bowl, hole puncher, folding ruler, vise, periscope, extension cord, musical cymbals, shoe stretcher, Lazy Susan, bottle brush, soldering iron, tambourine, tennis-racket press, knapsack, wood plane, balsa wood, movie reel, pipe wrench, radiator air valve, cabbage, glass cutter, various flowers in season. Even include some bird and animal calls you can imitate.

Estimation and measurement

This may sound like a mathematics program—and it is. But it is also part of science. Measurement and science experimentation go hand in hand. It is of great value in our lives to learn to estimate distances, weights, temperatures, time intervals. Why even last night, on TV a witness in a murder trial was asked how many yards away she was from the scene of the crime!

Make up introductions to show the importance of estimation at home, industry, play, or hobbies, both for boys and girls. Say that you are going to test everyone's ability in this field.

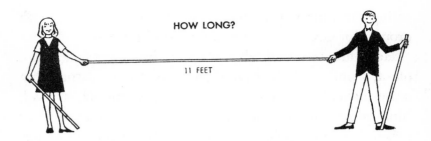

11 FEET

1. *HOW LONG?* Have several poles or ropes whose sizes are 20 inches, 5 feet, 11 feet or longer. Let two assistants hold the ends. Ask the audience to make silent guesses. Use a folding ruler to obtain the correct measurement. Tell it to everyone and find out who came closest to the answer.

2. *HOW HIGH?* How high is the auditorium flagpole? How high is the public-address loudspeaker? How high is the ceiling? Now, how can we find that out? We cannot throw up a little boy. He might get scared! Ask for suggestions on how to get up to the ceiling.

Try lashing together several sticks you have on stage. For a clever and laughter-producing device, you might have a hidden helium-filled balloon to send up. Do you only measure the vertical string? No! You must also include the diameter of the balloon.

There are many other ways to measure a high ceiling in an auditorium. Another method is to stand against the wall. Have someone from a distance estimate how many times taller the wall is than your height. In a real pinch, you might even ask the custodian to bring in his tallest ladder!

Also estimate the height of a short person and a tall person. After a while the audience gets caught in the excitement of this unusual program.

3. *HOW HEAVY?* Have cartons of various weights tied with strings for lifting. Use a scale on the stage for checking up on the estimates. How much does a certain friend weigh? Have someone try to pick you up to guess your weight. If a teacher or the principal is a good-natured fellow, have someone try to lift him for estimation. Great fun!

4. *WHAT TEMPERATURE?* Everybody guesses the temperature in the auditorium. Then have someone read a large thermometer you have on the stage. Ask if this is the temperature all over the room. Have several people check with thermometers, while you continue with the program. What is the temperature at the ceiling? If the blowers are not on, and there are no drafts, the ceiling temperature may be about 15 degrees or more higher than at the floor. Use long sticks, or your funny helium balloon, to send up your themometer. Take it down fast and read it quickly.

5. *HOW MANY SECONDS?* Clap your hands, wait, and then clap again. How many seconds have elapsed? Assistants check with their own watches or

with the school's stop watch.   Audiences usually miss
by a wide margin since they have had very little prac-

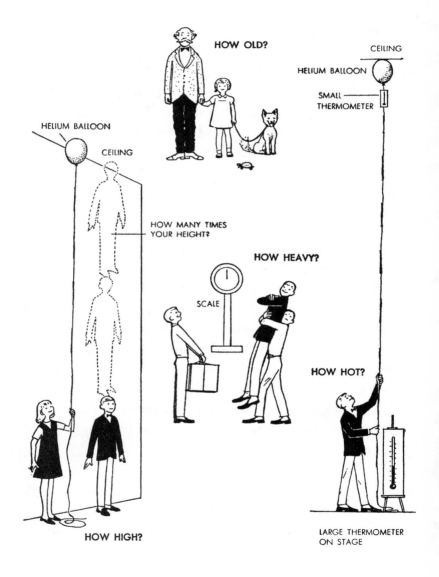

tice in this field. Teach everybody how to count seconds by reciting at conversational speed, "One thousand and one, one thousand and two, one thousand and three." Now repeat your time-estimation exercise, while everybody counts seconds *silently*. This time, many more will come close to the correct answer.

6. *HOW OLD?* Estimate ages of older men in the room. Ask them beforehand for permission. It is unbelievable how poorly youngsters estimate ages of older people.

7. *HOW MANY MILES?* Select nearby landmarks such as the public library, City Hall, the town square or park. Check up on the straight-line distances of these places from where you are. Use a map or mileage measurer on a car or bicycle.

8. *MORE IDEAS.* There are numerous other speeds, distances, volumes, temperatures, etc., which can be estimated. For example: How fast is one walking across the stage in miles per hour? How long will it take for a container to have its water emptied? How many marbles or beans in a jar? How cool is the water from the faucet? How old is the dog?

Portions of this program can become part of other kinds of science shows. Audiences enjoy being given opportunities to participate.

Inviting guest speakers

There are many scientific businesses and professions in which a friend or relative works. These people are often eager to talk to youngsters, and show them unusual instruments and demonstrations connected with their interesting occupations.

At first, only you should ask several provocative questions. Then you must allow the visitor to speak without many interruptions. When he is through, the audience can ask questions.

Politely caution the speaker to explain everything in simple terms, and not to talk above the educational level of his audience. Demonstration material should be visible to all. Supply him with a good microphone if necessary, and also good lighting conditions.

Tell him his time limit in advance, so he will not feel rushed. Thank him graciously at the end.

Build-it-yourself workshops

For small groups you can hand each one some inexpensive materials. With these they construct some scientific toy, instrument, or other device, which you demonstrate.

If some special items are needed, tell them in advance to find these, or purchase them, and to bring them to the meeting.

Using a classroom public-address system

Many schools today have a school-wide, public-address system. From a microphone in the principal's office, one can speak to students in every room. In many schools, short messages are heard daily, usually before classes start their work.

Ask the principal for two or three minutes of broadcast time. Write brief, scientific talks which will appeal to several grades, if not to the entire school. Make them breezy and informative. Avoid long, dull explanations. Below are some topics for delivery:

1. Discuss some very important scientific newspaper headline of the day. Explain the principle and importance to each student.
2. Tell how to spend an interesting weekend on a nature walk, visit to museum, doing a certain science experiment, etc.
3. Point out the science behind the work of plumbers, painters, or roofers now in the school.
4. Explain the reasons for changing to Daylight Saving Time. Try to inject humor into this topic.
5. Talk about the snow, hail, or thunderstorm that day.

6. Indicate how a knowledge of science might have avoided the accident in, or outside the school this morning.
7. Today is the first day of Spring!
8. Point out several excellent science programs on TV or radio.
9. Try to arouse interest in a science book you just read.
10. Explain the scientific principle behind a currently popular toy or game.

Index

A CATALOG OF SELECTED
DOVER BOOKS
IN ALL FIELDS OF INTEREST

A CATALOG OF SELECTED
DOVER BOOKS
IN ALL FIELDS OF INTEREST

DRAWINGS OF REMBRANDT, edited by Seymour Slive. Updated Lippmann, Hofstede de Groot edition, with definitive scholarly apparatus. All portraits, biblical sketches, landscapes, nudes. Oriental figures, classical studies, together with selection of work by followers. 550 illustrations. Total of 630pp. 9⅛ × 12¼.
21485-0, 21486-9 Pa., Two-vol. set $29.90

GHOST AND HORROR STORIES OF AMBROSE BIERCE, Ambrose Bierce. 24 tales vividly imagined, strangely prophetic, and decades ahead of their time in technical skill: "The Damned Thing," "An Inhabitant of Carcosa," "The Eyes of the Panther," "Moxon's Master," and 20 more. 199pp. 5⅜ × 8½. 20767-6 Pa. $4.95

ETHICAL WRITINGS OF MAIMONIDES, Maimonides. Most significant ethical works of great medieval sage, newly translated for utmost precision, readability. Laws Concerning Character Traits, Eight Chapters, more. 192pp. 5⅜ × 8½.
24522-5 Pa. $5.95

THE EXPLORATION OF THE COLORADO RIVER AND ITS CANYONS, J. W. Powell. Full text of Powell's 1,000-mile expedition down the fabled Colorado in 1869. Superb account of terrain, geology, vegetation, Indians, famine, mutiny, treacherous rapids, mighty canyons, during exploration of last unknown part of continental U.S. 400pp. 5⅜ × 8½. 20094-9 Pa. $8.95

HISTORY OF PHILOSOPHY, Julián Marías. Clearest one-volume history on the market. Every major philosopher and dozens of others, to Existentialism and later. 505pp. 5⅜ × 8½. 21739-6 Pa. $9.95

ALL ABOUT LIGHTNING, Martin A. Uman. Highly readable nontechnical survey of nature and causes of lightning, thunderstorms, ball lightning, St. Elmo's Fire, much more. Illustrated. 192pp. 5⅜ × 8½. 25237-X Pa. $5.95

SAILING ALONE AROUND THE WORLD, Captain Joshua Slocum. First man to sail around the world, alone, in small boat. One of great feats of seamanship told in delightful manner. 67 illustrations. 294pp. 5⅜ × 8½. 20326-3 Pa. $4.95

LETTERS AND NOTES ON THE MANNERS, CUSTOMS AND CONDITIONS OF THE NORTH AMERICAN INDIANS, George Catlin. Classic account of life among Plains Indians: ceremonies, hunt, warfare, etc. 312 plates. 572pp. of text. 6⅛ × 9¼. 22118-0, 22119-9, Pa., Two-vol. set $17.90

THE SECRET LIFE OF SALVADOR DALÍ, Salvador Dalí. Outrageous but fascinating autobiography through Dalí's thirties with scores of drawings and sketches and 80 photographs. A must for lovers of 20th-century art. 432pp. 6½ × 9¼. (Available in U.S. only) 27454-3 Pa. $9.95

CATALOG OF DOVER BOOKS

THE BOOK OF BEASTS: Being a Translation from a Latin Bestiary of the Twelfth Century, T. H. White. Wonderful catalog of real and fanciful beasts: manticore, griffin, phoenix, amphivius, jaculus, many more. White's witty erudite commentary on scientific, historical aspects enhances fascinating glimpse of medieval mind. Illustrated. 296pp. 5⅜ × 8¼. (Available in U.S. only)   24609-4 Pa. $7.95

FRANK LLOYD WRIGHT: Architecture and Nature with 160 Illustrations, Donald Hoffmann. Profusely illustrated study of influence of nature—especially prairie—on Wright's designs for Fallingwater, Robie House, Guggenheim Museum, other masterpieces. 96pp. 9¼ × 10¾.   25098-9 Pa. $8.95

LIMBERT ARTS AND CRAFTS FURNITURE: The Complete 1903 Catalog, Charles P. Limbert and Company. Rare catalog depicting 188 pieces of Mission-style furniture: fold-down tables and desks, bookcases, library and octagonal tables, chairs, more. Descriptive captions. 80pp. 9⅜ × 12¼.   27120-X Pa. $6.95

YEARS WITH FRANK LLOYD WRIGHT: Apprentice to Genius, Edgar Tafel. Insightful memoir by a former apprentice presents a revealing portrait of Wright the man, the inspired teacher, the greatest American architect. 372 black-and-white illustrations. Preface. Index. vi + 228pp. 8¼ × 11.   24801-1 Pa. $10.95

THE STORY OF KING ARTHUR AND HIS KNIGHTS, Howard Pyle. Enchanting version of King Arthur fable has delighted generations with imaginative narratives of exciting adventures and unforgettable illustrations by the author. 41 illustrations. xviii + 313pp. 6⅛ × 9¼.   21445-1 Pa. $6.95

THE GODS OF THE EGYPTIANS, E. A. Wallis Budge. Thorough coverage of numerous gods of ancient Egypt by foremost Egyptologist. Information on evolution of cults, rites and gods; the cult of Osiris; the Book of the Dead and its rites; the sacred animals and birds; Heaven and Hell; and more. 956pp. 6⅛ × 9¼.
22055-9, 22056-7 Pa., Two-vol. set $22.90

A THEOLOGICO-POLITICAL TREATISE, Benedict Spinoza. Also contains unfinished *Political Treatise*. Great classic on religious liberty, theory of government on common consent. R. Elwes translation. Total of 421pp. 5⅜ × 8½.
20249-6 Pa. $7.95

INCIDENTS OF TRAVEL IN CENTRAL AMERICA, CHIAPAS, AND YUCATAN, John L. Stephens. Almost single-handed discovery of Maya culture; exploration of ruined cities, monuments, temples; customs of Indians. 115 drawings. 892pp. 5⅜ × 8½.   22404-X, 22405-8 Pa., Two-vol. set $17.90

LOS CAPRICHOS, Francisco Goya. 80 plates of wild, grotesque monsters and caricatures. Prado manuscript included. 183pp. 6⅜ × 9⅜.   22384-1 Pa. $6.95

AUTOBIOGRAPHY: The Story of My Experiments with Truth, Mohandas K. Gandhi. Not hagiography, but Gandhi in his own words. Boyhood, legal studies, purification, the growth of the Satyagraha (nonviolent protest) movement. Critical, inspiring work of the man who freed India. 480pp. 5⅜ × 8½. (Available in U.S. only)
24593-4 Pa. $6.95

ILLUSTRATED DICTIONARY OF HISTORIC ARCHITECTURE, edited by Cyril M. Harris. Extraordinary compendium of clear, concise definitions for over 5,000 important architectural terms complemented by over 2,000 line drawings. Covers full spectrum of architecture from ancient ruins to 20th-century Modernism. Preface. 592pp. 7½ × 9⅝. 24444-X Pa. $15.95

THE NIGHT BEFORE CHRISTMAS, Clement C. Moore. Full text, and woodcuts from original 1848 book. Also critical, historical material. 19 illustrations. 40pp. 4⅝ × 6. 22797-9 Pa. $2.50

THE LESSON OF JAPANESE ARCHITECTURE: 165 Photographs, Jiro Harada. Memorable gallery of 165 photographs taken in the 1930s of exquisite Japanese homes of the well-to-do and historic buildings. 13 line diagrams. 192pp. 8⅜ × 11¼. 24778-3 Pa. $10.95

THE AUTOBIOGRAPHY OF CHARLES DARWIN AND SELECTED LETTERS, edited by Francis Darwin. The fascinating life of eccentric genius composed of an intimate memoir by Darwin (intended for his children); commentary by his son, Francis; hundreds of fragments from notebooks, journals, papers; and letters to and from Lyell, Hooker, Huxley, Wallace and Henslow. xi + 365pp. 5⅜ × 8. 20479-0 Pa. $6.95

WONDERS OF THE SKY: Observing Rainbows, Comets, Eclipses, the Stars and Other Phenomena, Fred Schaaf. Charming, easy-to-read poetic guide to all manner of celestial events visible to the naked eye. Mock suns, glories, Belt of Venus, more. Illustrated. 299pp. 5¼ × 8¼. 24402-4 Pa. $8.95

BURNHAM'S CELESTIAL HANDBOOK, Robert Burnham, Jr. Thorough guide to the stars beyond our solar system. Exhaustive treatment. Alphabetical by constellation: Andromeda to Cetus in Vol. 1; Chamaeleon to Orion in Vol. 2; and Pavo to Vulpecula in Vol. 3. Hundreds of illustrations. Index in Vol. 3. 2,000pp. 6⅛ × 9¼. 23567-X, 23568-8, 23673-0 Pa., Three-vol. set $41.85

STAR NAMES: Their Lore and Meaning, Richard Hinckley Allen. Fascinating history of names various cultures have given to constellations and literary and folkloristic uses that have been made of stars. Indexes to subjects. Arabic and Greek names. Biblical references. Bibliography. 563pp. 5⅜ × 8½. 21079-0 Pa. $9.95

THIRTY YEARS THAT SHOOK PHYSICS: The Story of Quantum Theory, George Gamow. Lucid, accessible introduction to influential theory of energy and matter. Careful explanations of Dirac's anti-particles, Bohr's model of the atom, much more. 12 plates. Numerous drawings. 240pp. 5⅜ × 8½. 24895-X Pa. $6.95

CHINESE DOMESTIC FURNITURE IN PHOTOGRAPHS AND MEASURED DRAWINGS, Gustav Ecke. A rare volume, now affordably priced for antique collectors, furniture buffs and art historians. Detailed review of styles ranging from early Shang to late Ming. Unabridged republication. 161 black-and-white drawings, photos. Total of 224pp. 8⅜ × 11¼. (Available in U.S. only) 25171-3 Pa. $14.95

VINCENT VAN GOGH: A Biography, Julius Meier-Graefe. Dynamic, penetrating study of artist's life, relationship with brother, Theo, painting techniques, travels, more. Readable, engrossing. 160pp. 5⅜ × 8½. (Available in U.S. only) 25253-1 Pa. $4.95

HOW TO WRITE, Gertrude Stein. Gertrude Stein claimed anyone could understand her unconventional writing—here are clues to help. Fascinating improvisations, language experiments, explanations illuminate Stein's craft and the art of writing. Total of 414pp. 4⅝ × 6⅜. 23144-5 Pa. $6.95

ADVENTURES AT SEA IN THE GREAT AGE OF SAIL: Five Firsthand Narratives, edited by Elliot Snow. Rare true accounts of exploration, whaling, shipwreck, fierce natives, trade, shipboard life, more. 33 illustrations. Introduction. 353pp. 5⅜ × 8½. 25177-2 Pa. $9.95

THE HERBAL OR GENERAL HISTORY OF PLANTS, John Gerard. Classic descriptions of about 2,850 plants—with over 2,700 illustrations—includes Latin and English names, physical descriptions, varieties, time and place of growth, more. 2,706 illustrations. xlv + 1,678pp. 8½ × 12¼. 23147-X Cloth. $89.95

DOROTHY AND THE WIZARD IN OZ, L. Frank Baum. Dorothy and the Wizard visit the center of the Earth, where people are vegetables, glass houses grow and Oz characters reappear. Classic sequel to *Wizard of Oz*. 256pp. 5⅜ × 8.
24714-7 Pa. $5.95

SONGS OF EXPERIENCE: Facsimile Reproduction with 26 Plates in Full Color, William Blake. This facsimile of Blake's original "Illuminated Book" reproduces 26 full-color plates from a rare 1826 edition. Includes "The Tyger," "London," "Holy Thursday," and other immortal poems. 26 color plates. Printed text of poems. 48pp. 5¼ × 7. 24636-1 Pa. $3.95

SONGS OF INNOCENCE, William Blake. The first and most popular of Blake's famous "Illuminated Books," in a facsimile edition reproducing all 31 brightly colored plates. Additional printed text of each poem. 64pp. 5¼ × 7.
22764-2 Pa. $3.95

PRECIOUS STONES, Max Bauer. Classic, thorough study of diamonds, rubies, emeralds, garnets, etc.: physical character, occurrence, properties, use, similar topics. 20 plates, 8 in color. 94 figures. 659pp. 6⅛ × 9¼.
21910-0, 21911-9 Pa., Two-vol. set $21.90

ENCYCLOPEDIA OF VICTORIAN NEEDLEWORK, S. F. A. Caulfeild and Blanche Saward. Full, precise descriptions of stitches, techniques for dozens of needlecrafts—most exhaustive reference of its kind. Over 800 figures. Total of 679pp. 8⅛ × 11. 22800-2, 22801-0 Pa., Two-vol. set $26.90

THE MARVELOUS LAND OF OZ, L. Frank Baum. Second Oz book, the Scarecrow and Tin Woodman are back with hero named Tip, Oz magic. 136 illustrations. 287pp. 5⅜ × 8½. 20692-0 Pa. $5.95

WILD FOWL DECOYS, Joel Barber. Basic book on the subject, by foremost authority and collector. Reveals history of decoy making and rigging, place in American culture, different kinds of decoys, how to make them, and how to use them. 140 plates. 156pp. 7⅞ × 10¾. 20011-6 Pa. $14.95

HISTORY OF LACE, Mrs. Bury Palliser. Definitive, profusely illustrated chronicle of lace from earliest times to late 19th century. Laces of Italy, Greece, England, France, Belgium, etc. Landmark of needlework scholarship. 266 illustrations. 672pp. 6⅛ × 9¼. 24742-2 Pa. $16.95

ILLUSTRATED GUIDE TO SHAKER FURNITURE, Robert Meader. All furniture and appurtenances, with much on unknown local styles. 235 photos. 146pp. 9 × 12.
22819-3 Pa. $9.95

WHALE SHIPS AND WHALING: A Pictorial Survey, George Francis Dow. Over 200 vintage engravings, drawings, photographs of barks, brigs, cutters, other vessels. Also harpoons, lances, whaling guns, many other artifacts. Comprehensive text by foremost authority. 207 black-and-white illustrations. 288pp. 6 × 9.
24808-9 Pa. $9.95

THE BERTRAMS, Anthony Trollope. Powerful portrayal of blind self-will and thwarted ambition includes one of Trollope's most heartrending love stories. 497pp. 5⅜ × 8½.
25119-5 Pa. $9.95

ADVENTURES WITH A HAND LENS, Richard Headstrom. Clearly written guide to observing and studying flowers and grasses, fish scales, moth and insect wings, egg cases, buds, feathers, seeds, leaf scars, moss, molds, ferns, common crystals, etc.—all with an ordinary, inexpensive magnifying glass. 209 exact line drawings aid in your discoveries. 220pp. 5⅜ × 8½.
23330-8 Pa. $5.95

RODIN ON ART AND ARTISTS, Auguste Rodin. Great sculptor's candid, wide-ranging comments on meaning of art; great artists; relation of sculpture to poetry, painting, music; philosophy of life, more. 76 superb black-and-white illustrations of Rodin's sculpture, drawings and prints. 119pp. 8⅜ × 11¼.
24487-3 Pa. $7.95

FIFTY CLASSIC FRENCH FILMS, 1912–1982: A Pictorial Record, Anthony Slide. Memorable stills from Grand Illusion, Beauty and the Beast, Hiroshima, Mon Amour, many more. Credits, plot synopses, reviews, etc. 160pp. 8¼ × 11.
25256-6 Pa. $11.95

THE PRINCIPLES OF PSYCHOLOGY, William James. Famous long course complete, unabridged. Stream of thought, time perception, memory, experimental methods; great work decades ahead of its time. 94 figures. 1,391pp. 5⅜ × 8½.
20381-6, 20382-4 Pa., Two-vol. set $25.90

BODIES IN A BOOKSHOP, R. T. Campbell. Challenging mystery of blackmail and murder with ingenious plot and superbly drawn characters. In the best tradition of British suspense fiction. 192pp. 5⅜ × 8½.
24720-1 Pa. $5.95

CALLAS: Portrait of a Prima Donna, George Jellinek. Renowned commentator on the musical scene chronicles incredible career and life of the most controversial, fascinating, influential operatic personality of our time. 64 black-and-white photographs. 416pp. 5⅜ × 8¼.
25047-4 Pa. $8.95

GEOMETRY, RELATIVITY AND THE FOURTH DIMENSION, Rudolph Rucker. Exposition of fourth dimension, concepts of relativity as Flatland characters continue adventures. Popular, easily followed yet accurate, profound. 141 illustrations. 133pp. 5⅜ × 8½.
23400-2 Pa. $4.95

HOUSEHOLD STORIES BY THE BROTHERS GRIMM, with pictures by Walter Crane. 53 classic stories—Rumpelstiltskin, Rapunzel, Hansel and Gretel, the Fisherman and his Wife, Snow White, Tom Thumb, Sleeping Beauty, Cinderella, and so much more—lavishly illustrated with original 19th-century drawings. 114 illustrations. x + 269pp. 5⅜ × 8½.
21080-4 Pa. $4.95

SUNDIALS, Albert Waugh. Far and away the best, most thorough coverage of ideas, mathematics concerned, types, construction, adjusting anywhere. Over 100 illustrations. 230pp. 5⅜ × 8½. 22947-5 Pa. $5.95

PICTURE HISTORY OF THE NORMANDIE: With 190 Illustrations, Frank O. Braynard. Full story of legendary French ocean liner: Art Deco interiors, design innovations, furnishings, celebrities, maiden voyage, tragic fire, much more. Extensive text. 144pp. 8⅞ × 11¾. 25257-4 Pa. $11.95

THE FIRST AMERICAN COOKBOOK: A Facsimile of "American Cookery," 1796, Amelia Simmons. Facsimile of the first American-written cookbook published in the United States contains authentic recipes for colonial favorites—pumpkin pudding, winter squash pudding, spruce beer, Indian slapjacks, and more. Introductory Essay and Glossary of colonial cooking terms. 80pp. 5⅜ × 8½. 24710-4 Pa. $3.50

101 PUZZLES IN THOUGHT AND LOGIC, C. R. Wylie, Jr. Solve murders and robberies, find out which fishermen are liars, how a blind man could possibly identify a color—purely by your own reasoning! 107pp. 5⅜ × 8½. 20367-0 Pa. $2.95

ANCIENT EGYPTIAN MYTHS AND LEGENDS, Lewis Spence. Examines animism, totemism, fetishism, creation myths, deities, alchemy, art and magic, other topics. Over 50 illustrations. 432pp. 5⅜ × 8½. 26525-0 Pa. $8.95

ANTHROPOLOGY AND MODERN LIFE, Franz Boas. Great anthropologist's classic treatise on race and culture. Introduction by Ruth Bunzel. Only inexpensive paperback edition. 255pp. 5⅜ × 8½. 25245-0 Pa. $7.95

THE TALE OF PETER RABBIT, Beatrix Potter. The inimitable Peter's terrifying adventure in Mr. McGregor's garden, with all 27 wonderful, full-color Potter illustrations. 55pp. 4¼ × 5½. 22827-4 Pa. $1.75

THREE PROPHETIC SCIENCE FICTION NOVELS, H. G. Wells. *When the Sleeper Wakes, A Story of the Days to Come* and *The Time Machine* (full version). 335pp. 5⅜ × 8½. (Available in U.S. only) 20605-X Pa. $8.95

APICIUS COOKERY AND DINING IN IMPERIAL ROME, edited and translated by Joseph Dommers Vehling. Oldest known cookbook in existence offers readers a clear picture of what foods Romans ate, how they prepared them, etc. 49 illustrations. 301pp. 6⅛ × 9¼. 23563-7 Pa. $8.95

SHAKESPEARE LEXICON AND QUOTATION DICTIONARY, Alexander Schmidt. Full definitions, locations, shades of meaning of every word in plays and poems. More than 50,000 exact quotations. 1,485pp. 6½ × 9¼. 22726-X, 22727-8 Pa., Two-vol. set $31.90

THE WORLD'S GREAT SPEECHES, edited by Lewis Copeland and Lawrence W. Lamm. Vast collection of 278 speeches from Greeks to 1970. Powerful and effective models; unique look at history. 842pp. 5⅜ × 8½. 20468-5 Pa. $12.95

THE BLUE FAIRY BOOK, Andrew Lang. The first, most famous collection, with many familiar tales: Little Red Riding Hood, Aladdin and the Wonderful Lamp, Puss in Boots, Sleeping Beauty, Hansel and Gretel, Rumpelstiltskin; 37 in all. 138 illustrations. 390pp. 5⅜ × 8½. 21437-0 Pa. $6.95

THE STORY OF THE CHAMPIONS OF THE ROUND TABLE, Howard Pyle. Sir Launcelot, Sir Tristram and Sir Percival in spirited adventures of love and triumph retold in Pyle's inimitable style. 50 drawings, 31 full-page. xviii + 329pp. 6½ × 9¼. 21883-X Pa. $7.95

THE MYTHS OF THE NORTH AMERICAN INDIANS, Lewis Spence. Myths and legends of the Algonquins, Iroquois, Pawnees and Sioux with comprehensive historical and ethnological commentary. 36 illustrations. 5⅜ × 8½.
25967-6 Pa. $8.95

GREAT DINOSAUR HUNTERS AND THEIR DISCOVERIES, Edwin H. Colbert. Fascinating, lavishly illustrated chronicle of dinosaur research, 1820s to 1960. Achievements of Cope, Marsh, Brown, Buckland, Mantell, Huxley, many others. 384pp. 5¼ × 8¼. 24701-5 Pa. $8.95

THE TASTEMAKERS, Russell Lynes. Informal, illustrated social history of American taste 1850s-1950s. First popularized categories Highbrow, Lowbrow, Middlebrow. 129 illustrations. New (1979) afterword. 384pp. 6 × 9.
23993-4 Pa. $8.95

NORTH AMERICAN INDIAN LIFE: Customs and Traditions of 23 Tribes, Elsie Clews Parsons (ed.). 27 fictionalized essays by noted anthropologists examine religion, customs, government, additional facets of life among the Winnebago, Crow, Zuni, Eskimo, other tribes. 480pp. 6⅛ × 9¼. 27377-6 Pa. $10.95

AUTHENTIC VICTORIAN DECORATION AND ORNAMENTATION IN FULL COLOR: 46 Plates from "Studies in Design," Christopher Dresser. Superb full-color lithographs reproduced from rare original portfolio of a major Victorian designer. 48pp. 9¼ × 12¼. 25083-0 Pa. $7.95

PRIMITIVE ART, Franz Boas. Remains the best text ever prepared on subject, thoroughly discussing Indian, African, Asian, Australian, and, especially, Northern American primitive art. Over 950 illustrations show ceramics, masks, totem poles, weapons, textiles, paintings, much more. 376pp. 5⅜ × 8. 20025-6 Pa. $8.95

SIDELIGHTS ON RELATIVITY, Albert Einstein. Unabridged republication of two lectures delivered by the great physicist in 1920-21. *Ether and Relativity* and *Geometry and Experience*. Elegant ideas in nonmathematical form, accessible to intelligent layman. vi + 56pp. 5⅜ × 8½. 24511-X Pa. $3.95

THE WIT AND HUMOR OF OSCAR WILDE, edited by Alvin Redman. More than 1,000 ripostes, paradoxes, wisecracks: Work is the curse of the drinking classes, I can resist everything except temptation, etc. 258pp. 5⅜ × 8½. 20602-5 Pa. $4.95

ADVENTURES WITH A MICROSCOPE, Richard Headstrom. 59 adventures with clothing fibers, protozoa, ferns and lichens, roots and leaves, much more. 142 illustrations. 232pp. 5⅜ × 8½. 23471-1 Pa. $4.95

CATALOG OF DOVER BOOKS

PLANTS OF THE BIBLE, Harold N. Moldenke and Alma L. Moldenke. Standard reference to all 230 plants mentioned in Scriptures. Latin name, biblical reference, uses, modern identity, much more. Unsurpassed encyclopedic resource for scholars, botanists, nature lovers, students of Bible. Bibliography. Indexes. 123 black-and-white illustrations. 384pp. 6 × 9. 25069-5 Pa. $9.95

FAMOUS AMERICAN WOMEN: A Biographical Dictionary from Colonial Times to the Present, Robert McHenry, ed. From Pocahontas to Rosa Parks, 1,035 distinguished American women documented in separate biographical entries. Accurate, up-to-date data, numerous categories, spans 400 years. Indices. 493pp. 6½ × 9¼. 24523-3 Pa. $11.95

THE FABULOUS INTERIORS OF THE GREAT OCEAN LINERS IN HISTORIC PHOTOGRAPHS, William H. Miller, Jr. Some 200 superb photographs capture exquisite interiors of world's great "floating palaces"—1890s to 1980s: *Titanic, Ile de France, Queen Elizabeth, United States, Europa*, more. Approx. 200 black-and-white photographs. Captions. Text. Introduction. 160pp. 8⅜ × 11¼. 24756-2 Pa. $10.95

THE GREAT LUXURY LINERS, 1927–1954: A Photographic Record, William H. Miller, Jr. Nostalgic tribute to heyday of ocean liners. 186 photos of *Ile de France, Normandie, Leviathan, Queen Elizabeth, United States,* many others. Interior and exterior views. Introduction. Captions. 160pp. 9 × 12. 24056-8 Pa. $12.95

A NATURAL HISTORY OF THE DUCKS, John Charles Phillips. Great landmark of ornithology offers complete detailed coverage of nearly 200 species and subspecies of ducks: gadwall, sheldrake, merganser, pintail, many more. 74 full-color plates, 102 black-and-white. Bibliography. Total of 1,920pp. 8⅜ × 11¼. 25141-1, 25142-X Cloth., Two-vol. set $100.00

THE COMPLETE "MASTERS OF THE POSTER": All 256 Color Plates from "Les Maîtres de l'Affiche", Stanley Appelbaum (ed.). The most famous compilation ever made of the art of the great age of the poster, featuring works by Chéret, Steinlen, Toulouse-Lautrec, nearly 100 other artists. One poster per page. 272pp. 9¼ × 12¼. 26309-6 Pa. $29.95

THE TEN BOOKS OF ARCHITECTURE: The 1755 Leoni Edition, Leon Battista Alberti. Rare classic helped introduce the glories of ancient architecture to the Renaissance. 68 black-and-white plates. 336pp. 8⅜ × 11¼. 25239-6 Pa. $14.95

MISS MACKENZIE, Anthony Trollope. Minor masterpieces by Victorian master unmasks many truths about life in 19th-century England. First inexpensive edition in years. 392pp. 5⅜ × 8½. 25201-9 Pa. $8.95

THE RIME OF THE ANCIENT MARINER, Gustave Doré, Samuel Taylor Coleridge. Dramatic engravings considered by many to be his greatest work. The terrifying space of the open sea, the storms and whirlpools of an unknown ocean, the ice of Antarctica, more—all rendered in a powerful, chilling manner. Full text. 38 plates. 77pp. 9¼ × 12. 22305-1 Pa. $4.95

THE EXPEDITIONS OF ZEBULON MONTGOMERY PIKE, Zebulon Montgomery Pike. Fascinating firsthand accounts (1805–6) of exploration of Mississippi River, Indian wars, capture by Spanish dragoons, much more. 1,088pp. 5⅜ × 8½. 25254-X, 25255-8 Pa., Two-vol. set $25.90

CATALOG OF DOVER BOOKS

A CONCISE HISTORY OF PHOTOGRAPHY: Third Revised Edition, Helmut Gernsheim. Best one-volume history—camera obscura, photochemistry, daguerreotypes, evolution of cameras, film, more. Also artistic aspects—landscape, portraits, fine art, etc. 281 black-and-white photographs. 26 in color. 176pp. 8⅜ × 11¼.
25128-4 Pa. $14.95

THE DORÉ BIBLE ILLUSTRATIONS, Gustave Doré. 241 detailed plates from the Bible: the Creation scenes, Adam and Eve, Flood, Babylon, battle sequences, life of Jesus, etc. Each plate is accompanied by the verses from the King James version of the Bible. 241pp. 9 × 12. 23004-X Pa. $9.95

WANDERINGS IN WEST AFRICA, Richard F. Burton. Great Victorian scholar/adventurer's invaluable descriptions of African tribal rituals, fetishism, culture, art, much more. Fascinating 19th-century account. 624pp. 5⅜ × 8½. 26890-X Pa. $12.95

HISTORIC HOMES OF THE AMERICAN PRESIDENTS, Second Revised Edition, Irvin Haas. Guide to homes occupied by every president from Washington to Bush. Visiting hours, travel routes, more. 175 photos. 160pp. 8¼ × 11.
26751-2 Pa. $9.95

THE HISTORY OF THE LEWIS AND CLARK EXPEDITION, Meriwether Lewis and William Clark, edited by Elliott Coues. Classic edition of Lewis and Clark's day-by-day journals that later became the basis for U.S. claims to Oregon and the West. Accurate and invaluable geographical, botanical, biological, meteorological and anthropological material. Total of 1,508pp. 5⅜ × 8½.
21268-8, 21269-6, 21270-X Pa., Three-vol. set $29.85

LANGUAGE, TRUTH AND LOGIC, Alfred J. Ayer. Famous, clear introduction to Vienna, Cambridge schools of Logical Positivism. Role of philosophy, elimination of metaphysics, nature of analysis, etc. 160pp. 5⅜ × 8½. (Available in U.S. and Canada only) 20010-8 Pa. $3.95

MATHEMATICS FOR THE NONMATHEMATICIAN, Morris Kline. Detailed, college-level treatment of mathematics in cultural and historical context, with numerous exercises. For liberal arts students. Preface. Recommended Reading Lists. Tables. Index. Numerous black-and-white figures. xvi + 641pp. 5⅜ × 8½.
24823-2 Pa. $11.95

HANDBOOK OF PICTORIAL SYMBOLS, Rudolph Modley. 3,250 signs and symbols, many systems in full; official or heavy commercial use. Arranged by subject. Most in Pictorial Archive series. 143pp. 8⅛ × 11. 23357-X Pa. $8.95

INCIDENTS OF TRAVEL IN YUCATAN, John L. Stephens. Classic (1843) exploration of jungles of Yucatan, looking for evidences of Maya civilization. Travel adventures, Mexican and Indian culture, etc. Total of 669pp. 5⅜ × 8½.
20926-1, 20927-X Pa., Two-vol. set $13.90

DEGAS: An Intimate Portrait, Ambroise Vollard. Charming, anecdotal memoir by famous art dealer of one of the greatest 19th-century French painters. 14 black-and-white illustrations. Introduction by Harold L. Van Doren. 96pp. 5⅜ × 8½.
25131-4 Pa. $4.95

PERSONAL NARRATIVE OF A PILGRIMAGE TO AL–MADINAH AND MECCAH, Richard F. Burton. Great travel classic by remarkably colorful personality. Burton, disguised as a Moroccan, visited sacred shrines of Islam, narrowly escaping death. 47 illustrations. 959pp. 5⅜ × 8½.
21217-3, 21218-1 Pa., Two-vol. set $19.90

PHRASE AND WORD ORIGINS, A. H. Holt. Entertaining, reliable, modern study of more than 1,200 colorful words, phrases, origins and histories. Much unexpected information. 254pp. 5⅜ × 8½.
20758-7 Pa. $5.95

THE RED THUMB MARK, R. Austin Freeman. In this first Dr. Thorndyke case, the great scientific detective draws fascinating conclusions from the nature of a single fingerprint. Exciting story, authentic science. 320pp. 5⅜ × 8½. (Available in U.S. only)
25210-8 Pa. $6.95

AN EGYPTIAN HIEROGLYPHIC DICTIONARY, E. A. Wallis Budge. Monumental work containing about 25,000 words or terms that occur in texts ranging from 3000 B.C. to 600 A.D. Each entry consists of a transliteration of the word, the word in hieroglyphs, and the meaning in English. 1,314pp. 6⅜ × 10.
23615-3, 23616-1 Pa., Two-vol. set $35.90

THE COMPLEAT STRATEGYST: Being a Primer on the Theory of Games of Strategy, J. D. Williams. Highly entertaining classic describes, with many illustrated examples, how to select best strategies in conflict situations. Prefaces. Appendices. xvi + 268pp. 5⅜ × 8½.
25101-2 Pa. $7.95

THE ROAD TO OZ, L. Frank Baum. Dorothy meets the Shaggy Man, little Button-Bright and the Rainbow's beautiful daughter in this delightful trip to the magical Land of Oz. 272pp. 5⅜ × 8.
25208-6 Pa. $5.95

POINT AND LINE TO PLANE, Wassily Kandinsky. Seminal exposition of role of point, line, other elements in nonobjective painting. Essential to understanding 20th-century art. 127 illustrations. 192pp. 6½ × 9¼.
23808-3 Pa. $5.95

LADY ANNA, Anthony Trollope. Moving chronicle of Countess Lovel's bitter struggle to win for herself and daughter Anna their rightful rank and fortune—perhaps at cost of sanity itself. 384pp. 5⅜ × 8½.
24669-8 Pa. $8.95

EGYPTIAN MAGIC, E. A. Wallis Budge. Sums up all that is known about magic in Ancient Egypt: the role of magic in controlling the gods, powerful amulets that warded off evil spirits, scarabs of immortality, use of wax images, formulas and spells, the secret name, much more. 253pp. 5⅜ × 8½.
22681-6 Pa. $4.95

THE DANCE OF SIVA, Ananda Coomaraswamy. Preeminent authority unfolds the vast metaphysic of India: the revelation of her art, conception of the universe, social organization, etc. 27 reproductions of art masterpieces. 192pp. 5⅜ × 8½.
24817-8 Pa. $6.95

CHRISTMAS CUSTOMS AND TRADITIONS, Clement A. Miles. Origin, evolution, significance of religious, secular practices. Caroling, gifts, yule logs, much more. Full, scholarly yet fascinating; non-sectarian. 400pp. 5⅜ × 8½.
23354-5 Pa. $7.95

THE HUMAN FIGURE IN MOTION, Eadweard Muybridge. More than 4,500 stopped-action photos, in action series, showing undraped men, women, children jumping, lying down, throwing, sitting, wrestling, carrying, etc. 390pp. 7⅞ × 10⅝.
20204-6 Cloth. $24.95

THE MAN WHO WAS THURSDAY, Gilbert Keith Chesterton. Witty, fast-paced novel about a club of anarchists in turn-of-the-century London. Brilliant social, religious, philosophical speculations. 128pp. 5⅜ × 8½.
25121-7 Pa. $3.95

A CÉZANNE SKETCHBOOK: Figures, Portraits, Landscapes and Still Lifes, Paul Cézanne. Great artist experiments with tonal effects, light, mass, other qualities in over 100 drawings. A revealing view of developing master painter, precursor of Cubism. 102 black-and-white illustrations. 144pp. 8¾ × 6⅜.
24790-2 Pa. $6.95

AN ENCYCLOPEDIA OF BATTLES: Accounts of Over 1,560 Battles from 1479 B.C. to the Present, David Eggenberger. Presents essential details of every major battle in recorded history, from the first battle of Megiddo in 1479 B.C. to Grenada in 1984. List of Battle Maps. New Appendix covering the years 1967–1984. Index. 99 illustrations. 544pp. 6½ × 9¼.
24913-1 Pa. $14.95

AN ETYMOLOGICAL DICTIONARY OF MODERN ENGLISH, Ernest Weekley. Richest, fullest work, by foremost British lexicographer. Detailed word histories. Inexhaustible. Total of 856pp. 6½ × 9¼.
21873-2, 21874-0 Pa., Two-vol. set $19.90

WEBSTER'S AMERICAN MILITARY BIOGRAPHIES, edited by Robert McHenry. Over 1,000 figures who shaped 3 centuries of American military history. Detailed biographies of Nathan Hale, Douglas MacArthur, Mary Hallaren, others. Chronologies of engagements, more. Introduction. Addenda. 1,033 entries in alphabetical order. xi + 548pp. 6½ × 9¼. (Available in U.S. only)
24758-9 Pa. $13.95

LIFE IN ANCIENT EGYPT, Adolf Erman. Detailed older account, with much not in more recent books: domestic life, religion, magic, medicine, commerce, and whatever else needed for complete picture. Many illustrations. 597pp. 5⅜ × 8½.
22632-8 Pa. $9.95

HISTORIC COSTUME IN PICTURES, Braun & Schneider. Over 1,450 costumed figures shown, covering a wide variety of peoples: kings, emperors, nobles, priests, servants, soldiers, scholars, townsfolk, peasants, merchants, courtiers, cavaliers, and more. 256pp. 8⅜ × 11¼.
23150-X Pa. $9.95

THE NOTEBOOKS OF LEONARDO DA VINCI, edited by J. P. Richter. Extracts from manuscripts reveal great genius; on painting, sculpture, anatomy, sciences, geography, etc. Both Italian and English. 186 ms. pages reproduced, plus 500 additional drawings, including studies for *Last Supper, Sforza* monument, etc. 860pp. 7⅞ × 10¾.
22572-0, 22573-9 Pa., Two-vol. set $35.90

THE ART NOUVEAU STYLE BOOK OF ALPHONSE MUCHA: All 72 Plates from "Documents Decoratifs" in Original Color, Alphonse Mucha. Rare copyright-free design portfolio by high priest of Art Nouveau. Jewelry, wallpaper, stained glass, furniture, figure studies, plant and animal motifs, etc. Only complete one-volume edition. 80pp. 9⅜ × 12¼. 24044-4 Pa. $10.95

ANIMALS: 1,419 Copyright-Free Illustrations of Mammals, Birds, Fish, Insects, Etc., edited by Jim Harter. Clear wood engravings present, in extremely lifelike poses, over 1,000 species of animals. One of the most extensive pictorial sourcebooks of its kind. Captions. Index. 284pp. 9 × 12. 23766-4 Pa. $10.95

OBELISTS FLY HIGH, C. Daly King. Masterpiece of American detective fiction, long out of print, involves murder on a 1935 transcontinental flight—"a very thrilling story"—*NY Times*. Unabridged and unaltered republication of the edition published by William Collins Sons & Co. Ltd., London, 1935. 288pp. 5⅜ × 8½. (Available in U.S. only) 25036-9 Pa. $5.95

VICTORIAN AND EDWARDIAN FASHION: A Photographic Survey, Alison Gernsheim. First fashion history completely illustrated by contemporary photographs. Full text plus 235 photos, 1840–1914, in which many celebrities appear. 240pp. 6½ × 9¼. 24205-6 Pa. $8.95

THE ART OF THE FRENCH ILLUSTRATED BOOK, 1700–1914, Gordon N. Ray. Over 630 superb book illustrations by Fragonard, Delacroix, Daumier, Doré, Grandville, Manet, Mucha, Steinlen, Toulouse-Lautrec and many others. Preface. Introduction. 633 halftones. Indices of artists, authors & titles, binders and provenances. Appendices. Bibliography. 608pp. 8⅜ × 11¼. 25086-5 Pa. $24.95

THE WONDERFUL WIZARD OF OZ, L. Frank Baum. Facsimile in full color of America's finest children's classic. 143 illustrations by W. W. Denslow. 267pp. 5⅜ × 8½. 20691-2 Pa. $7.95

FOLLOWING THE EQUATOR: A Journey Around the World, Mark Twain. Great writer's 1897 account of circumnavigating the globe by steamship. Ironic humor, keen observations, vivid and fascinating descriptions of exotic places. 197 illustrations. 720pp. 5⅜ × 8½. 26113-1 Pa. $15.95

THE FRIENDLY STARS, Martha Evans Martin & Donald Howard Menzel. Classic text marshalls the stars together in an engaging, nontechnical survey, presenting them as sources of beauty in night sky. 23 illustrations. Foreword. 2 star charts. Index. 147pp. 5⅜ × 8½. 21099-5 Pa. $3.95

FADS AND FALLACIES IN THE NAME OF SCIENCE, Martin Gardner. Fair, witty appraisal of cranks, quacks, and quackeries of science and pseudoscience: hollow earth, Velikovsky, orgone energy, Dianetics, flying saucers, Bridey Murphy, food and medical fads, etc. Revised, expanded In the Name of Science. "A very able and even-tempered presentation."—*The New Yorker.* 363pp. 5⅜ × 8. 20394-8 Pa. $6.95

ANCIENT EGYPT: Its Culture and History, J. E. Manchip White. From predynastics through Ptolemies: society, history, political structure, religion, daily life, literature, cultural heritage. 48 plates. 217pp. 5⅜ × 8½. 22548-8 Pa. $5.95

SIR HARRY HOTSPUR OF HUMBLETHWAITE, Anthony Trollope. Incisive, unconventional psychological study of a conflict between a wealthy baronet, his idealistic daughter, and their scapegrace cousin. The 1870 novel in its first inexpensive edition in years. 250pp. 5⅜ × 8½.   24953-0 Pa. $6.95

LASERS AND HOLOGRAPHY, Winston E. Kock. Sound introduction to burgeoning field, expanded (1981) for second edition. Wave patterns, coherence, lasers, diffraction, zone plates, properties of holograms, recent advances. 84 illustrations. 160pp. 5⅜ × 8¼. (Except in United Kingdom)   24041-X Pa. $4.95

INTRODUCTION TO ARTIFICIAL INTELLIGENCE: Second, Enlarged Edition, Philip C. Jackson, Jr. Comprehensive survey of artificial intelligence—the study of how machines (computers) can be made to act intelligently. Includes introductory and advanced material. Extensive notes updating the main text. 132 black-and-white illustrations. 512pp. 5⅜ × 8½.   24864-X Pa. $10.95

HISTORY OF INDIAN AND INDONESIAN ART, Ananda K. Coomaraswamy. Over 400 illustrations illuminate classic study of Indian art from earliest Harappa finds to early 20th century. Provides philosophical, religious and social insights. 304pp. 6⅜ × 9⅜.   25005-9 Pa. $11.95

THE GOLEM, Gustav Meyrink. Most famous supernatural novel in modern European literature, set in Ghetto of Old Prague around 1890. Compelling story of mystical experiences, strange transformations, profound terror. 13 black-and-white illustrations. 224pp. 5⅜ × 8½.   25025-3 Pa. $7.95

PICTORIAL ENCYCLOPEDIA OF HISTORIC ARCHITECTURAL PLANS, DETAILS AND ELEMENTS: With 1,880 Line Drawings of Arches, Domes, Doorways, Facades, Gables, Windows, etc., John Theodore Haneman. Sourcebook of inspiration for architects, designers, others. Bibliography. Captions. 141pp. 9 × 12.   24605-1 Pa. $8.95

BENCHLEY LOST AND FOUND, Robert Benchley. Finest humor from early 30s, about pet peeves, child psychologists, post office and others. Mostly unavailable elsewhere. 73 illustrations by Peter Arno and others. 183pp. 5⅜ × 8½.   22410-4 Pa. $4.95

ERTÉ GRAPHICS, Erté. Collection of striking color graphics: *Seasons, Alphabet, Numerals, Aces* and *Precious Stones.* 50 plates, including 4 on covers. 48pp. 9⅜ × 12¼.   23580-7 Pa. $7.95

THE JOURNAL OF HENRY D. THOREAU, edited by Bradford Torrey, F. H. Allen. Complete reprinting of 14 volumes, 1837–61, over two million words; the sourcebooks for *Walden,* etc. Definitive. All original sketches, plus 75 photographs. 1,804pp. 8½ × 12¼.   20312-3, 20313-1 Cloth., Two-vol. set $130.00

CASTLES: Their Construction and History, Sidney Toy. Traces castle development from ancient roots. Nearly 200 photographs and drawings illustrate moats, keeps, baileys, many other features. Caernarvon, Dover Castles, Hadrian's Wall, Tower of London, dozens more. 256pp. 5⅜ × 8¼.   24898-4 Pa. $7.95

CATALOG OF DOVER BOOKS

AMERICAN CLIPPER SHIPS: 1833–1858, Octavius T. Howe & Frederick C. Matthews. Fully-illustrated, encyclopedic review of 352 clipper ships from the period of America's greatest maritime supremacy. Introduction. 109 halftones. 5 black-and-white line illustrations. Index. Total of 928pp. 5⅜ × 8½.
25115-2, 25116-0 Pa., Two-vol. set $21.90

TOWARDS A NEW ARCHITECTURE, Le Corbusier. Pioneering manifesto by great architect, near legendary founder of "International School." Technical and aesthetic theories, views on industry, economics, relation of form to function, "mass-production spirit," much more. Profusely illustrated. Unabridged translation of 13th French edition. Introduction by Frederick Etchells. 320pp. 6⅛ × 9¼. (Available in U.S. only)
25023-7 Pa. $8.95

THE BOOK OF KELLS, edited by Blanche Cirker. Inexpensive collection of 32 full-color, full-page plates from the greatest illuminated manuscript of the Middle Ages, painstakingly reproduced from rare facsimile edition. Publisher's Note. Captions. 32pp. 9⅜ × 12¼. (Available in U.S. only)
24345-1 Pa. $5.95

BEST SCIENCE FICTION STORIES OF H. G. WELLS, H. G. Wells. Full novel *The Invisible Man*, plus 17 short stories: "The Crystal Egg," "Aepyornis Island," "The Strange Orchid," etc. 303pp. 5⅜ × 8½. (Available in U.S. only)
21531-8 Pa. $6.95

AMERICAN SAILING SHIPS: Their Plans and History, Charles G. Davis. Photos, construction details of schooners, frigates, clippers, other sailcraft of 18th to early 20th centuries—plus entertaining discourse on design, rigging, nautical lore, much more. 137 black-and-white illustrations. 240pp. 6⅛ × 9¼.
24658-2 Pa. $6.95

ENTERTAINING MATHEMATICAL PUZZLES, Martin Gardner. Selection of author's favorite conundrums involving arithmetic, money, speed, etc., with lively commentary. Complete solutions. 112pp. 5⅜ × 8½.
25211-6 Pa. $3.95

THE WILL TO BELIEVE, HUMAN IMMORTALITY, William James. Two books bound together. Effect of irrational on logical, and arguments for human immortality. 402pp. 5⅜ × 8½.
20291-7 Pa. $8.95

THE HAUNTED MONASTERY and THE CHINESE MAZE MURDERS, Robert Van Gulik. 2 full novels by Van Gulik continue adventures of Judge Dee and his companions. An evil Taoist monastery, seemingly supernatural events; overgrown topiary maze that hides strange crimes. Set in 7th-century China. 27 illustrations. 328pp. 5⅜ × 8½.
23502-5 Pa. $6.95

CELEBRATED CASES OF JUDGE DEE (DEE GOONG AN), translated by Robert Van Gulik. Authentic 18th-century Chinese detective novel; Dee and associates solve three interlocked cases. Led to Van Gulik's own stories with same characters. Extensive introduction. 9 illustrations. 237pp. 5⅜ × 8½.
23337-5 Pa. $5.95

Prices subject to change without notice.

Available at your book dealer or write for free catalog to Dept. GI, Dover Publications, Inc., 31 East 2nd St., Mineola, N.Y. 11501. Dover publishes more than 400 books each year on science, elementary and advanced mathematics, biology, music, art, literary history, social sciences and other areas.